How to Succeed in the 21st Century

D1445528

How to Succeed in the 21st Century

FOCUS ON THE THINGS OVER WHICH YOU HAVE INPUT, IMPACT AND CONTROL

Ned Grossman

Diamond Publishing Company
Cleveland, Ohio

ISBN: 978-0-692-05562-5

Diamond Publishing Company
Cleveland, Ohio
www.nedgrossman.com

To Sheri, for who you were and
for what you left behind.

To Jenny and Adam, for who you are.

To Noah, Sadie, Stella, and Luiza,
for who you will become.

To Shelly . . . and Lisa and Amy,
for who you are.

Contents

How to
Succeed
in the
21st Century

Preface

Almost a quarter century ago (1994!), I wrote *How To Succeed in Life: Ideas and Principles They Don't Teach in School*. It was dedicated to my two wonderful children, Jennifer, then 17, and Adam, then 15.

The dedication read:

> *When you were born, I had three wishes for you:*
> - *To be healthy*
> - *To become independent*
> - *To experience the thrill, excitement and joy of a Championship sports team in Cleveland.*

Happily, as they were then, Jenny and Adam are both healthy and independent. And, while it took 22 years, they have now experienced the excitement and joy of a Championship team in Cleveland. Thank you, 2015–2016 Cleveland Cavaliers!

My first book took more than 10 years to write. Fortunately, I was under no time pressure and thoroughly enjoyed the project. It was a personal labor of love: something that I wanted to do, committed to doing, and did.

Initially, I intended to print just two copies: one for Jenny; one for Adam. I quickly learned that it didn't cost much more to print 500 copies than it did to print only two. Now, almost twenty-five years later, there have been eight printings and nearly 50,000 copies in print! A major school book distributor purchased 10,000; a national marketing organization purchased 10,000; school Superintendents have given them to their graduating seniors as they walked across the stage to receive their diplomas; senior corporate executives have given them to their employees. All this happened with almost no marketing effort and no coast-to-coast book tour. I shamelessly admit that I am very pleased and proud with the book's ongoing, wide-spread acceptance. I am flattered, knowing the impact the book has had on so many people in widely diverse areas. I can honestly say that if I were offered millions of dollars to recall all my books, I wouldn't consider it, not even for a moment.

Throughout life, we are always trying to teach our children life's valuable lessons that we hope they will remember and use to their benefit. I wrote the book with the hope and feeling that, if my kids read the book and followed its laws and principles, they could achieve anything they wanted. Did the book have the intended effect on Jenny and Adam? I definitely think so.

Jenny is enjoying a terrific life as an exemplary daughter, wife, and mother. She had an illustrious career as a National Account Manager for a major insurance company. Now, in addition to her extensive volunteer activities, she is a highly successful sales consultant for a prominent worldwide cosmetics company. She was featured in a story about successful sales representatives and gave this advice:

- Believe in yourself.
- Trust your gut.
- Learn from your mistakes.
- YOU control your own destiny.

Obviously, I'm very proud of my daughter. Her advice is FABULOUS and works not only for industrious and ambitious young people, but it applies to everyone!

Adam is enjoying a terrific life as an exemplary son, husband, and father. He has a successful career with the Boston Red Sox. After graduating from college, he began as an intern, became an integral part of the organization, and is now their Chief Marketing Officer. He is the proud recipient of three Boston Red Sox World Series championship rings!

When interviewed by a Boston newspaper, Adam was asked, "Who was an influential mentor in your life and what did he teach you?" I was flattered that Adam picked me, his dad. He recalled these pearls of paternal wisdom:

- Can't doesn't exist.
- There is no substitute for hard work.
- It's better having everyone in the room thinking you're stupid than opening your mouth and proving it.
- There is no bad time for a nap.
- Follow your passion, and things will turn out well.

While I believe my book influenced both Jenny and Adam, I readily admit that THE smartest decision my kids ever made was to emulate their mother, Sheri. Unfortunately, Sheri passed away nine years ago after a long and heroic battle with pancreatic cancer. Living in Sheri's image, inspired by her memory and following her teachings, both Jenny and Adam are leading remarkable lives and are admired as role models by a plethora of friends and colleagues.

This book is a second effort to provide additional, simple, easy-to-understand thoughts and suggestions on how to successfully lead your life in today's world. The basic principles and philosophies haven't changed, but the rapidly changing world, and my advancing age, have created new perspectives, new thoughts, new ideas, and new learning opportunities. I am not a life coach, personal trainer, nutritionist, social worker, psychologist, psychiatrist, or Ph.D. I am a retired employee benefits consultant who has passionately studied "How to Succeed in Life" for over 50 years.

You won't find newfound science or technological thoughts or revelations. It is a compilation of a lifetime of research, reading, study, and experience. Much of this timeless material you may have heard before.

Intended as a manual of basic, fundamental guidelines, this book does not have to be read in any particular order. Initially, open randomly to any page. Read a short passage and give it thoughtful contemplation. See if the thoughts make sense. Consider keeping the book readily accessible and using it as a friendly reference.

The quotes have been carefully researched for correctness and attribution. The others are used with gratitude to those who created them. Almost all the quotes have a male reference: "A man who . . . " "He who . . . " The quotations also "include" women and if they were written today they would be gender-inclusive. They would say, "People who . . . " or refer to "he or she."

For thousands of years, the sages have taught, and recorded, the paths to success and happiness. Today, we do not have to "reinvent the wheel" or "learn the hard way." We can easily read the writings of the "sages of the ages," study and understand their philosophies, and implement their time-tested teachings.

As you read this book, I hope you will find it interesting and provocative. May it encourage you to "Focus on the things over which YOU have Input, Impact, and Control." It's simple, but not easy.

CHAPTER 1

The Principles and Laws Don't Change

The December 19, 2016 issue of *Sports Illustrated* named Cleveland Cavaliers basketball legend LeBron James "Sportsperson of the Year." Not only is LeBron a once-in-a-generation, unmatched athlete, he is also blessed with uncommon wisdom. LeBron said:

> Life is like a book, and I think you have to go back and read your book sometimes to learn from it. Maybe I'm at Chapter 8 right now, but you can't sit down and start reading a book at Chapter 8. You have to go back to Chapter 1.

LeBron's provocative comment inspired me to go back and reread my own book, "How To Succeed in Life, Ideas and Principles They Don't Teach in School." Rereading it reinforced my strong thoughts, feelings, and convictions that life's really important principles, laws, and rules haven't changed. The supposed "secrets of the universe" are anything but secrets. They remain constant elements in nature's laws and have existed since the beginning of recorded time.

SANSKRIT

Approximately 4,500 years ago, it was written in Sanskrit:

Look well to this one day, for it and it alone is life.

*In the brief course of this day lie all the
verities and realities of your existence*

*Yesterday is only a dream, and
tomorrow is but a vision.*

*Yet each day, well lived, makes every
yesterday a dream of happiness*

*Look well, therefore, to this day,
for it and it alone is life.*

How often have we heard, and been told, "one day at a time?" Clearly, this most basic philosophy is not a new idea.

TAO TE CHING

Fast forward 2,000 years. Lao-Tzu's classic book, the *Tao Te Ching*, (pronounced Dow Deh Jing) or "Book of the Way," is an ancient manual concisely depicting the art of living. It is one of the unsung wonders of the world. Written around 500 B.C.E., it has been called the wisest book ever written. Next to the Bible, it is the most widely translated book in world literature and is the basis for Taoism, which is a system of beliefs, attitudes, and practices that encourages a person to simply accept oneself.

Little is known about Lao-Tzu, but he may have been a contemporary of Confucius, 551–479 B.C.E. In 81 very succinct chapters, the book examines the basic predicament of being alive. It gives advice and imparts balance and perspective in an effort to create a serene and generous spirit. Here are excerpts from Stephen Mitchell's 1988 translation. After careful reflection, you might be inspired to read the entire book. It doesn't take long.

Chapter 3:   Practice not-doing, and everything will fall into place.

Chapter 8:   In dwelling, live close to the ground.

In thinking, keep to the simple.

In conflict, be fair and generous.

In governing, don't try to control.

In work, do what you enjoy.

In family life, be completely present.

When you are content to be simply yourself and don't compare or compete, everybody will respect you.

Chapter 11:   We shape clay into a pot, but it is the emptiness inside that holds whatever we want.

We hammer wood for a house, but it is the inner space that makes it livable.

Chapter 13:   Have faith in the way things are.

Chapter 16: Immersed in the wonder of the Tao, you can deal with whatever life brings you, and when death comes, you are ready.

Chapter 24: . . . just do your job, then let go.

Chapter 29: Do you want to improve the world? I don't think it can be done . . . The Master sees things as they are, without trying to control them.

Chapter 30: Because he believes in himself, he doesn't try to convince others. Because he is content with himself, he doesn't need others' approval.

Because he accepts himself, the whole world accepts him.

Chapter 33: Knowing others is intelligence; knowing yourself is wisdom.

Mastering others is strength, mastering yourself is true power. If you realize that you have enough, you are truly rich.

Chapter 42: Ordinary people hate solitude. But the Master makes use of it, embracing his aloneness, realizing he is one with the whole universe.

Chapter 44: Be content with what you have; rejoice in the way things are.

When you realize there is nothing lacking, the whole world belongs to you.

Chapter 45:   The Master allows things to happen.

Chapter 47:   The more you know, the less you understand.

Chapter 48:   True mastery can be gained by letting things go their own way. It cannot be gained by interfering.

Chapter 56:   Those who know don't talk. Those who talk don't know.

Chapter 64:   The giant pine tree grows from a tiny sprout.

The journey of a thousand miles starts from beneath your feet.

Chapter 67:   I have just three things to teach:

Simplicity, patience, compassion.

These three are your greatest treasures.

Simple in actions and in thoughts you return to the source of being.

Patient with both friends and enemies, you accord with the way things are.

Compassionate toward yourself, you reconcile all beings in the world.

Fabulous! Right? Please remember that these words of wisdom and internal peace were written approximately 2,500 years ago.

CLASSIC WISDOM

During the nineteenth century, three of America's most revered and respected thinkers offered a myriad of thoughts and wisdom. They are quoted frequently throughout this book. Here are three of their best:

What the mind of man can conceive
and believe, it can achieve.
—Napoleon Hill, 1883–1970

If one advances confidently in the direction
of his dreams, and endeavors to lead the life
which he has imagined, he will meet with a
success unexpected in common hours.
—Henry David Thoreau, 1817–1862

Finish each day and be done with it. You have done
what you could. Some blunders and absurdities have
crept in; forget them as soon as you can. Tomorrow is a
new day. You shall begin it serenely and with too high
a spirit to be encumbered with your old nonsense.
—Ralph Waldo Emerson, 1803–1882

MODERN WISDOM

Now, fast forward to 1965, the year I graduated from college. Even with a freshly minted business degree, I had absolutely no idea what I wanted to do with my life. I was confused, frustrated, and discouraged . . . lost. Fred Heinlen, my former high school baseball coach, mentor, and friend, gave me a set of audiocassette tapes by Earl Nightingale entitled: "Lead the Field." Fred suggested I might get valuable information from Earl's lifelong research into what makes people successful. I agreed to listen to the tapes, not because I thought they would be helpful, but as an accommodation to a good friend. I thought: "If the 'secrets of success' could be summarized in a series of audiocassette tapes, why didn't everybody listen, learn, and utilize these principles and become successful?"

Taking Fred's advice and listening to those tapes was one of the most dramatic things I ever did. The tapes provided a clear focus for my life and put me on the road to achieving everything I had always wanted. I learned that the "secrets" of the universe are not secrets at all. The paths to success have already been clearly documented. Even in today's rapidly changing, highly technological world, all we have to do is read the advice of our wise predecessors and follow their proven principles, ideas, and rules. For all he did for me and for all the wisdom he imparted over five decades, I am forever indebted to Fred Heinlen.

Earl Nightingale (1921-1989)

Earl Nightingale's insights became the basis for my first book. They are as true today as they were 50 years ago. Here are some of the most valuable ideas I learned from Earl Nightingale:

We become what we think about.

It is our attitude at the beginning of a difficult undertaking which, more than anything else, will determine our success or failure.

Success is the progressive realization of a worthy ideal.

To be what we are, and become what we are
capable of becoming, is the only end to life.
—Robert Louis Stevenson

Successful people are dreamers who have found their
dream too exciting, too important, to remain in the
realm of fantasy. Day by day, hour by hour, they toil
in the service of their dream until they can see it with
their eyes and touch it with their hands. A lifetime
consists of years, months, weeks, and days. The basic
unit of a lifetime is a single day. We need only to
perform successfully each act of a single day to enjoy
a successful day. If you can create a mental image of
the person you would most like to become, begin now
to act as that person would act in everything you do.
Gradually, imperceptibly, you'll become that person.
Your life will not be transformed overnight; there will
be no sudden miracle; but steadily day by day you
will grow into the image you hold in your mind.

While alive, live. The way you live is by sorting
out what it is you most enjoy doing, what
most interests you, and then do that.

When you know what you want, and you want
it badly enough, you'll find a way to get it.
—Jim Rohn

Everything operates on the law of cause and
effect: good cause, good effect; bad cause,
bad effect. That's why life is dull only to dull
people; effect can only mirror the cause.

*No one can become rich in any way without
enriching others. Anyone who adds to
prosperity must prosper in return.*

Give more than you receive in everything you do.

*The quest for excellence gives dignity to a
person. It gives character to a business. It gives
satisfaction to customers. It's still the surest way
to greatness, the unfailing road to success.*

*The happiest and most contented people are those who
each day perform, each day, to the best of their ability.*

*The happiest people are not the people
without problems; they are the people who
know how to solve their problems.*

*Most people fail not because they lack intelligence,
ability, opportunity or talent, but because they
haven't given their problem all they've got.*
—Robert H. Schuler

*Any person who produces less than his very best is
cheating. And, as Emerson was fond of pointing
out, in the long haul he only cheats himself.*

*Everything in the universe is just exactly the way
it is supposed to be. And what's the proof? It is.*

Dr. Wayne Dyer (1940-2015)

Wayne Dyer has been a major inspiration to me for more
than five decades. I immersed myself in his philosophies,
teachings, and stories. I loved his books, his audiocassette

tapes, his fundraising appearances on PBS, and his simple, easy to understand, practical, effective way of communicating.

Wayne's message is every bit as profound today as it was fifty years ago. In *Getting There,* Sara Blakely, 46-year-old Spanx inventor, said this: "When I was 16, my dad handed me Dr. Wayne Dyer's ten-tape series 'How to Be a No-Limit Person' and said, 'I wish someone had given this to me when I was your age.' I now tell people that one of the most important things they can do for themselves and their children is to listen to that series. Society constantly assaults us with negative images and messages. You have to go out of your way to view things in a positive light. Listening to 'How to Be a No-Limit Person' is my method. It has been emotionally encouraging, gotten me through the toughest of times, framed my thinking in a way that helped lead to the success of Spanx. I still listen to it a couple of times a year."

Here are some memorable Wayne Dyer quotes:

Peace is the result of retraining your mind to process life as it is, rather than as you think it should be.

You are not what you do. If you are what you do, then when you don't, you aren't. You are not what you do. Your worth as a human being does not come from your successes. Value doesn't come from what you accomplish. Your value is not determined by whether or not you win. If you have to win in order to have value, then somebody else has to lose. And that somebody else who is losing is determining whether you are a winner or not.

You are not what you do. You are what you believe about yourself. Your value doesn't come from anything but what you choose to think. Your corner of freedom is the willingness and the ability to think anything you want. That's yours. No one can change that for you. One of the most important things to learn in life is the sense of appreciation for yourself.

Remind yourself that you cannot fail at being yourself.

What other people think of me is none of my business. One of the highest places you can get is being independent of the good opinions of other people.

You don't need to be better than anyone else; you just need to be better than you used to be.

The main purpose in life is to enjoy it. If you learn how to enjoy your life, every moment you have, even the bad ones, you could never be a burden to anyone. Isn't that wonderful? Isn't that the least selfish thing you can do? Never be anybody else's burden! It's not selfish to know how to enjoy your life. It's selfless.

Every human being has a right to live their life as they choose to do as long as they don't interfere with anyone else's right to do the same.

Doing what you love is the cornerstone of having abundance in your life.

Generosity is a function of the heart, not of the wallet.

It's never crowded along the extra mile.

Look for solutions, not problems.

From all this classic wisdom, it should be absolutely clear that to lead happy, successful, rewarding lives, we must "Focus on the things over which WE have Input, Impact, and Control." Here is a basic list of the controllable and not controllable factors in our lives:

Controllable	Not Controllable
Our attitude	Weather
Our time	Sports scores
Our thoughts	Stock market
Our exercise	World politics
Our nutritional intake	
Our personal goals	

It is crucial to understand that the word "our" is associated with every topic over which we have Input, Impact, and Control. We must concentrate and devote our time and energy to these matters. The others, while interesting, important, provocative and controversial, are far outside our realm of impactful influence. No matter how many conversations we have with other people, regardless of how much time we spend watching sports, the weather and the news, we have almost no impact on those matters.

♦ ♦ ♦

Covering a period of 4,500 years (!), these legendary thinkers and philosophers, these icons, all espouse the same basic philosophies. They teach us how to think and act, and gently guide us along our own paths. They all teach that we can accomplish anything we want. Why? Because we each possess the requisite Input, Impact and Control. All we have to do is: "Just Do It!"

Focus on the things over which you have Input, Impact, and Control.

CHAPTER 2
Two Things Everybody Wants

HAPPINESS

There is no way to happiness. Happiness is the way.
—Thich Nhat Hanh

We already possess all the necessary ingredients for happiness: our minds, our bodies, our health, our family, and our friends. Most of these things came to us free, as standard equipment, when we were born. So make up YOUR mind to be happy NOW, today and every day.

Happiness is not something you ever arrive at. It is not a station in life. It is a way of traveling and is comprised of many tiny successes. Happiness is not what you have but how you enjoy what you do have. The happiest people are usually the busiest, most productive people who perform to the best of their ability every day.

Selected Thoughts on Happiness

Plenty of people miss their share of happiness
not because they never found it, but
because they didn't stop to enjoy it.
—William Feather

The happiness of life is made up of minute
fractions—the little, soon forgotten charities
of a kiss or a smile, a kind look, a heartfelt
compliment, and the countless infinitesimals
of pleasurable thought and genial feeling.
—Samuel Taylor Coleridge

To realize that true happiness can be achieved by
merely enjoying the simplest things in life.
To wake up every morning feeling blessed and
to live each moment as if it was our last.
—As seen on a sign at Awasi Hotel, Patagonia

Those who are happiest are those
who do the most for others.
—Booker T. Washington

To be happy, strive strenuously, daily,
unremittingly, to make others happy.
—B.C. Forbes

It is the very pursuit of happiness
that thwarts happiness.
—Viktor Frankel

If you want others to be happy, practice compassion.
If you want to be happy, practice compassion.
—Dalai Lama

*Your success and happiness lie in you. External
conditions are the accidents of life, its outer
trappings. The great enduring realities are love
of service. Joy is the holy fire that keeps our
purpose warm and our intelligence a glow.
Resolve to keep happy, and your joy and you
shall form an invincible host against difficulty.*
—Helen Keller

*When a happy person enters the room, it is
as if another candle has been lighted.*
—Carol Vanderheyden

SUCCESS

*There is only one success: to be able to
spend your life in your own way.*
—Christopher Morley

What a beautiful, simple concept! If you are doing what you enjoy, what makes you comfortable, what makes you feel good, what makes you happy, then you are successful. What more could you want?

Success does not automatically equate to wealth or status. Success has nothing to do with what other people think about you or your actions. It has only to do with YOUR own opinions of yourself and what YOU are doing. If you can enjoy each day fully and make your life work on your own terms and with your own sense of accomplishment and fulfillment, what more can you ask for?

My two favorite definitions of success are:

- Leading your life in your own way.
- The progressive realization of a worthy ideal.

Success is not magic; it is not a matter of luck. Success is a matter of habit. We can develop successful habits, live them daily, and master them. We can study how and why other people are successful and then adopt those habits and philosophies for ourselves.

If there is a shortcut to success, it is to learn from others. (See Chapter 11, Surround Yourself with Good People.) Do not waste time reinventing the wheel. Examine the life and behavior of everyone you encounter. Emulate the good. Reject the bad.

It is critical to success, happiness, and your personal sense of contentment and satisfaction to know, realistically, who you are and to completely understand your strengths and weaknesses in all areas of your life.

You have to accept your:

- Physical attributes: your stature, your height and weight
- Athletic, musical, artistic, technological abilities
- Educational background and training
- Work experiences
- Financial position
- Other factors over which you have NO input, impact, and control

Within that framework of understanding and acceptance, we have to factor in our passion and our innate abilities. Over the years, I have been privileged to speak to school children of various ages. Whenever I ask: "How many of you would like to become professional athletes?" at least half the students raise their hands. Is that goal possible? Obviously not.

Their desire is understandable but definitely not reasonable. The probability of any one student becoming a professional athlete is infinitesimal. So, I suggest to them: "Go for it and work extremely hard, but . . . understand the reality you face, and create your own back-up plan. Continue in school, get a college degree, prepare yourself for a more readily obtainable career: teacher, nurse, computer technician, lawyer, chef, landscaper . . . you name it. There are a lot more people in these very important careers than there are professional athletes."

When you face obstacles in life (diseases, addictions, rejections, unforeseen surprises of all kinds), first remember that no one is exempt from negative circumstances and unforeseen life events. Then consider implementing "The Six A's of Successfully Navigating Life's Path:"

- Awareness
- Acknowledgment
- Acceptance
- Adjustment
- Affirmation
- Action

A specific example is a negative habit. No matter how this habit occurred, or who is responsible and whom you want to blame, ultimately there is only one person who can solve the problem: YOU! The resolution may not be fast, simple, or easy, but the process is clear and, if applied judiciously, it will work:

- You have to be "aware" that you have a problem.
- You have to "acknowledge," at least to yourself, that the situation does exist.
- You have to "accept" the circumstances. You don't have to like them, but you have to "accept" them.
- You have to "adjust" your life to incorporate the necessary problem-solving techniques.
- You have to "affirm" your personal commitment to resolution.
- You have to "act."

This real-life situation, and suggested resolution, incorporates three very basic philosophies you will read about extensively in other chapters.

- Simplistic Solutions to Complicated Problems (SSCP)
- The KISS Principle (Keep It Short and Simple)
- Just Do It!

In 2002, Mark Shapiro, former General Manager and CEO of the Cleveland Indians, summed up his philosophy of "What It Takes for Success:"

- *It boils down to the basics.*
- *Hiring good solid people.*
- *Treating them as peers.*
- *Empowering them to make decisions.*
- *Backing them up after they've made them.*
- *Allowing them to shine.*
- *It's about creating an organization that lasts long after you've gone.*

The proof of Mark's sage comments came in 2016, a year after he left Cleveland to become CEO of the Toronto Blue Jays. The Indians, the team he helped create and mold, won the American League pennant and made it to the World Series for the first time in almost twenty years!

Selected Thoughts on Success

That man is a success who has lived well, laughed often and loved much; who has gained the respect of intelligent men and the love of children; who has filled his niche and accomplished his task; who leaves the world better than he found it, whether by an improved poppy, or a perfect poem or a rescued soul; who never lacked appreciation of earth's beauty or failed to express it; who looked for the best in others and gave the best he had.
—Robert Louis Stevenson

A successful person is one who went ahead and did the things the rest of us never quite got around to.

You can be successful and be honest. You can be successful and be ethical. You can be successful and keep your values. In other words, you can be successful and stand for what's right.
—J.C. Watts

The secret of success is constancy of purpose.
—Benjamin Disraeli

Let us be thankful for the fools. But for them, the rest of us could not succeed.
—Mark Twain

Never let success get to your head; never let failure get to your heart.
—Zaid K. Abdelnour

Success is doing what you like and making a living at it.

People rarely succeed at anything unless they have fun in what they are doing.
—Dale Carnegie

Focus on the things over which you have Input, Impact, and Control.

CHAPTER 3

How to Achieve Happiness and Success

THE RESPONSIBILITY IS OURS

You should accept absolute responsibility for your life and your success because, as you know, it is not luck, fate, the stars, heredity, circumstances, the economy, the weather, your spouse, your parents, or your boss. It is you. You are responsible for what you are and what you will become. To many people, that's threatening. But the truth is, we're all self-made, even though only the successful will admit it.
—Joel Weldon

That quote is one of my all-time favorites! Please read it again. Embrace it. Our futures are in our own hands and our own control. We have choices. We decide. We determine our own lives. Whatever we have inside us is not the result of what anybody else put there. We are the sum total of the choices we make in life. We cannot always control what goes on outside of us, but we can always control what goes on in our heads. We can control our thoughts and manage our emotions.

♦ ♦ ♦

Often I hear people say, *She's the way she is because when she was young, her mother did such and such.* Or, *He's the way he is because when he was a baby, his father did this or that.*

Those statements may be absolutely true. Yes, those parental actions did have input and impact on the individual's development. But those historical actions, whether ten, forty or fifty years ago, are not the overriding cause of what that person is today. Decades have passed. Other opportunities, experiences, and influences have come and gone. Children have grown to be adults. They have had years to take responsibilities for their own actions and for what they have, or have not, become. In his memoir, "Hillbilly Elegy," J.D. Vance summed it up: "No person's childhood gives him or her a perpetual moral, get-out-of-jail free card. At some point, you have to stop making excuses and take responsibility."

Your past is over and cannot be changed. You can remember it, love it or hate it, and even wish that it had been different. But all the wishing and blaming in the world will not change it. Responsibility means "to respond with ability." You have to say to yourself, "That is what happened in the past. I may not like it, but I cannot change it. Here is where I am in life today. Where do I want to be tomorrow, next week, and next year? Now how do I go about getting there?"

If we do not like something about ourselves, we have the choice of changing it. Consider that your life consists of the series of choices you have made, you are making, and you will continue to make.

Once you take absolute responsibility for your circumstances, those circumstances begin to improve. Eliminate excuses. Decide what kind of experiences you want to have. Become accountable to yourself. You will find yourself becoming more persistent, more courageous, and more determined. What you can do is phenomenal. But you must completely understand that almost everything that will ever happen to you is up to you.

It is important to note that sometimes "stuff" (sickness, illness, accidents) happens that is beyond our specific "input, impact and control." Nevertheless, it is how we choose to accept and deal with this unexpected "stuff" that helps us create as positive an outcome as possible.

Selected Thoughts on Responsibility

Every human being is responsible for himself and not under the obligation to meet the expectations of others.
—Fritz Perls

I am responsible for who I am.
—Neville Frankel

If you don't like how things are, change it. You're not a tree.
—Jim Rohn

More people would learn from their mistakes
if they weren't so busy denying them.
—Harold J. Smith

The most worthwhile endeavor I have
ever undertaken is responsibility for my
own life. It's hard, and it's worth it.
—LeVar Burton

You have absolute control over but one thing, and
that is your thoughts. If you fail to control your own
mind, you may be sure you will control nothing else.
—Napoleon Hill

It is not the situation that makes the man,
but the man who makes the situation.
—Frederick William Robertson

Our lives are about the choices we make every day.
Our destiny unfolds according to those choices.

Nothing is more responsible for the good
old days than a bad memory.
—Franklin P. Adams

OPPORTUNITY IS EVERYWHERE

Unless a man has trained himself for his chance,
the chance will only make him ridiculous.
—William Matthews

The fabled story of "Acres of Diamonds" is one of my all-time favorites. It tells of an African farmer who heard about people who had made huge fortunes discovering diamond mines. He wanted to be rich, so he sold his farm and spent the rest of his life in the fruitless pursuit of African diamonds. Broke, despondent, and desperate, he eventually threw himself in a river and drowned.

Meanwhile, the man who had bought the farm found a large stone in the stream that crossed his property. The stone turned out to be an enormously valuable diamond. He quickly discovered that his farm was covered with "acres of diamonds" and soon he became the owner of one of the world's richest diamond mines.

The first farmer had owned, literally, "acres of diamonds" but had sold them for practically nothing in order to look for them elsewhere. The obvious moral of the story is "The grass is not always greener on the other side of the road." Before leaving your present city, career, job, or relationship, examine them carefully. Be absolutely certain they do not contain all the opportunities, assets, and requisites you seek. If other pastures look greener, perhaps it is because they are getting better care!

Selected Thoughts on Opportunity

The secret of success in life is for a man to be
ready for his opportunity when it comes.
—Benjamin Disraeli

Believe that whenever one door closes, two doors open.

wWise men make more opportunities than they find.
—Francis Bacon

*Opportunity is missed by most people because
it is dressed in overalls and looks like work.*
—Thomas Edison

*Opportunity can be spelled with four letters. But
these letters are not L-U-C-K. They are W-O-R-K.*
—B. C. Forbes

SIX RULES FOR WINNING
THE "GAME OF LIFE"

I have coined an expression about the Game of Life: "You tell me what the rules are, and I'll figure out how to play the game."

This philosophy applies to all games (sports, cards, board), speed limits, laws (tax, immigration, etc.) Other people, organizations, or governments may make the rules, but we have the opportunity to study those rules and consciously decide how we can interpret, utilize, and implement them to our best advantage. Then we can then play the requisite game (legally, ethically, and morally) to achieve OUR most advantageous results. Given the rules, we have the Input, Impact and Control over how we choose to play the game.

And what is the most obvious, the most important game we play every day? It's the Game of Life. It can be played and won—just like baseball, bridge, or chess. Unfortunately, many of us spend our entire lifetime playing the all-important Game of Life without ever learning the rules!

Here are six important rules for achieving success and happiness and winning the Game of Life:

1. **We Become What We Think About.** If there is a "secret" for success and happiness, it is those six words. Realize that you can control what you think about and how you act accordingly. As Ralph Waldo Emerson said: "A man is what he thinks about all day long."

2. **Decide Exactly What You Want.** Decide exactly what career you want; exactly where you want to go to school; exactly how much money you want to earn; exactly where you want to live. These objectives must be clearly established in your mind before you can begin to make them happen. You can create the situations you want and, to a very great degree, control their outcomes.

3. **Determine the Price You Will Have to Pay.** The price is not necessarily measured in dollars. The cost is hard work, dedication, persistence, patience and determination. You must understand that you always have to pay the full price—there are no discounts, shortcuts or bargains—and you have to pay in advance.

4. **Commit to Pay the Price.** Your commitment must be absolute—no deviations, no excuses. When you completely commit to accomplishing exactly what you want, the answers to "how" and "when" will eventually unfold. They will come to you.

5. **Work Hard, One Day at a Time.** Try to live successfully, one day at a time. A successful life is nothing more than many successful days strung together. One successful day at a time will carry you over every hurdle. William James said, "Let no person worry about the success of his efforts. If you will do each day as best you can the work which is before you, you will wake up one day and find yourself one of the competent ones of your generation."

6. **Never Give Up!** No one is immune from everyday problems, but "When the going gets tough, the tough get going." We need to develop the ability to persevere in the face of adversity. When asked the key to success, the legendary British Prime Minister Winston Churchill summed it up in these words, "Never give up. Never, never, never give up."

Here is a very identifiable "Never Give Up" example. It is Abraham Lincoln's 30-year road to the White House.

1831 - Failed in business
1832 - Defeated for Legislature
1833 - Second failure in business
1836 - Suffered nervous breakdown
1838 - Defeated for Speaker
1840 - Defeated for Elector
1843 - Defeated for Congress
1848 - Defeated for Congress
1854 - Defeated for Senate
1856 - Defeated for Vice-President
1858 - Defeated for Senate
1860 - ELECTED PRESIDENT OF THE UNITED STATES

We have the input, impact, and control over the choices we make daily. We can choose to stop, "throw in the towel," quit, and give up. Or we can choose the mental toughness and control to "Never Give Up."

Selected Thoughts on Winning
"The Game of Life"

You have to learn the rules of the game. And then, you have to play better than anyone else.
—Albert Einstein

To get where you want to go, you must keep on keeping on.
—Norman Vincent Peale

Persistence and determination alone are omnipotent.
—Calvin Coolidge

Winners never quit and quitters never win.
—Vince Lombardi

People do not lack strength, they lack will.
—Victor Hugo

The difference between winning and losing is most often not quitting.
—Walt Disney

One of the things I learned the hard way was that it doesn't pay to get discouraged. Keeping busy and making optimism a way of life can restore your faith in yourself.
—Lucille Ball

Remember the tea kettle. Though up to its
neck in hot water, it continues to sing.

Continuous effort—not strength or intelligence—is
the key to unlocking and using our potential.
—Liane Cardes

You don't have to see the full staircase.
Just take the first step.
—Dr. Martin Luther King, Jr.

**Focus on the things over which you
have Input, Impact, and Control.**

CHAPTER 4
Our Most Important Assets

To accomplish what we want, attain all our goals, and achieve the success we deserve, we have to fully maximize our most important assets. Those assets are NOT our money, our education, our job, or our tangible personal property. Everything really worthwhile in our lives came to us free: our minds, hearts, bodies, souls, intelligence, dreams, ambitions, aspirations, and attitude. We need to appreciate our irreplaceable and priceless assets and maximize them every day.

How can we best utilize our invaluable assets? There are a myriad of books and audio sources by highly qualified professionals with years of experience and expertise in health, fitness, exercise, nutrition, etc. Here is a crash course in the most basic concepts.

ATTITUDE

The greatest discovery of my generation
is that human beings can alter their lives
by altering their attitudes of mind.
—William James

Fortunately, we control our own attitudes. We can decide if they are positive or negative. Positive attitudes yield positive results. Negative attitudes yield negative results. Here are two ideas to create positive attitudes:

- It is your attitude at the beginning of a task that more than anything else will influence its successful outcome.
- Your attitude toward others determines their attitude toward you.

Obviously, we can't control the weather, the traffic, the mood of people around us or what they think. But we can control our attitudes toward these events and these people. We all have the ability to determine what we think about in any given moment. No matter what happens to us, we have the ability to choose our response to the situation. By controlling what and how we think, we begin to control our own destinies.

Treat everyone you meet as the most important person on earth. Why? Because this is the way human beings should treat one another. And, as far as that person is concerned, he or she is the most important person on earth. People will give their love, affection, respect, support, and business to the person who treats them with appropriate dignity and respect. Try this idea for 30 days. See what kind of results you achieve! You won't go back to any other way of interacting with people.

Selected Thoughts on Attitude

The three most important words in the English language are 1. Attitude; 2. Attitude; 3. Attitude.
—Sherwood Strodel

Everything can be taken from a man but one thing: the last of the human freedoms— to choose one's attitude in any given set of circumstances, to choose one's own way.
—Viktor Frankel

It is our attitude toward events, not the events themselves, which we can control.
—Epictetus

It is not what happens to you, but how you react to it that matters.
—Epictetus

To accomplish great things, we must not only act, but also dream; not only plan, but also believe.
—Anatole France

If you change the way you look at things, the things that you look at will change.
—Wayne Dyer

*There is the positive side and the negative
side and at every moment, I decide.*
—William James

*There is very little difference in people, but that
little difference makes a big difference. The
little difference is attitude. The big difference
is whether it is positive or negative.*
—W. Clement Stone

*Keep your dreams alive. Understand to achieve
anything requires faith and belief in yourself, vision,
hard work, determination, and dedication. Remember
all things are possible for those who believe.*
—Gail Devers

*If you don't like something, change it. If you
can't change it, change your attitude.*
—Maya Angelou

*The tougher the fight, the more
important the mental attitude.*
—Michael Landon

*If you realized how powerful your thoughts are,
you would never think a negative thought.*
—Peace Pilgrim

HEALTH, FITNESS, AND EXERCISE

Good people strengthen themselves ceaselessly.
—Confucius

We all need to learn to take care of ourselves and our bodies. No one can do it for us!

Your body deserves and demands daily attention. It is surprising how little exercise it takes to keep your mind, heart, and body in good shape. Regular daily exercise will help you feel better, help you manage stress, keep you looking young and fit, and add years to your life. A workout is a personal triumph over laziness and procrastination. Don't be upset by the results you don't get with the workout you didn't do! Take action. An inch of movement will bring you closer to your goals than a mile of intention. As it is said: Use it or lose it!

The fittest people don't have the most time. They just make the best use of the time they have. Fitness has no age restrictions. Just get up and move! We get ourselves mentally and physically fit "one day at a time." We lose weight "one day at a time." No matter how smart we are or how much we wish, we can't speed up these processes. No matter how much money we have, we can't hire someone to work out for us. WE have to "Just Do It!"

For me, the best time for physical activity is first thing in the morning. It works both mentally and physically. Once

I have completed my workout, I know I have accomplished the most important thing in life: taking care of my mind and my body. Whatever else happens during the rest of the day, I know I have my priorities straight. I took care of myself first.

Selected Thoughts on Health and Fitness

Those who do not find time for exercise
will have to find time for illness.
—Edward Stanley

A person doesn't stop exercising because he gets too
old; he gets too old because he stops exercising.
—Kenneth Cooper, MD

You don't have to be sick to get better.
—Michael Josephson

He who has health has hope; and he
who has hope has everything.
—Thomas Carlyle

Your body is your container, not what you are.
—Emily Boorstein

Better keep yourself clean and bright.
You are the window through which
you must see the world.
—George Bernard Shaw

The secret to living well and living longer is: eat half,
walk double, laugh triple, love without measure.
—Tibetan proverb

NUTRITION

In a sincere effort to lose weight, we have all resolved to "go on a diet." The fact is we are always "on a diet." Our diet is what we eat every day. If we eat the "right" foods in the "right" proportions at the "right" time, our weight will usually take care of itself.

If we are really serious about losing weight, we need to be completely honest with ourselves about what we are eating every day. We don't have to eat less; we have to eat right. It is the law of cause and effect. Give your car the prescribed fuel, and it will run smoothly and efficiently. Similarly, give your body the right food, and it too will run smoothly and efficiently.

A helpful hint: If you don't have junk food in the house, you can't eat it! (SSCP: Simplistic Solution to a Complex Problem.) If you don't have cookies, candy, and ice cream in the house, you will have removed some of the temptation and most of the convenience. When you do have the perfectly natural craving for a tasty snack, it simply won't be there. You'll have to make it or go to the store to get it.

My nutritional inspiration and good friend, Julie DiBiasio, has created her own Ten Commandments of Healthy Living:

1. **Thou shall sleep.** Get plenty of rest and sleep. Sleep helps the body replenish itself. When you are sleep deprived, the body craves calorie-dense, sugar-filled, foods for quick energy.

2. **Thou shall move.** Moving helps us sleep better, builds strong bones and muscles, and reduces stress.

3. **Thou shall always drink water.** The formula for liquid intake is: your body weight x .67 = appropriate ounces per day.

4. **Thou shall incorporate vegetables or fruit with every meal.** Vegetables are better than fruit, but fruit will do.

5. **Thou shall live an 80/20 lifestyle.** Make 80% good food choices; 20% fun choices. We can't be perfect, so don't deprive yourself of the occasional fun snack.

6. **Thou shall limit refined sugar.** Refined sugar is an addiction. Stop it before it starts.

7. **Thou shall eat fat.** Nuts and hummus are good for you in moderation.

8. **Thou shall be an ingredient snob.** Read everything on the label. Try to buy things with five or fewer ingredients, all of which you can pronounce.

9. **Thou shall make lasting personal connections.** Spend time with family and friends who will help lift you up and make you happy.

10. **Thou shall have fun!** Do whatever makes you feel joy . . . in appropriate moderation.

In general, since the improvement of cookery,
mankind eats twice as much as nature requires.
—Benjamin Franklin

STRESS MANAGEMENT

The world seems to become more frenetic every day. We are continuously bombarded with more and more "things" we are supposed to understand, accomplish, and manage. It's no wonder we feel more "stressed." How do we deal with this ever-increasingly complex world? We should try to relax, slow down, take deep breaths, enjoy every moment, and become calmer and more serene.

Socrates suggested that the greatest gift in life is leisure. Leisure does not mean doing nothing or being lazy. It means taking a deep breath and trying to be relaxed, peaceful, in charge of our lives, and at ease doing what we enjoy doing. In difficult situations, realize and understand:

- The most stressful situations are the unresolved.
- One door closes, two doors open.
- It may be the end of a chapter, not the end of the book.
- Let it unfold.

The most stressful situations are the unresolved: marital conflicts, business disagreements, having too much to do in too short a time. As soon as these situations come to a resolution, the air is out of the balloon, people relax, and life proceeds on a less stressful course.

Everything in life has a purpose. The everything that doesn't go the way we expected or wanted has its own lesson, its own meaning. Embrace these situations for what they teach us.

Selected Thoughts on Stress Management

*Change happens when the pain of holding on
becomes greater than the fear of letting go.*
—Spencer Johnson

*Your temper is one of your most valuable
possessions. Don't lose it.*

REST AND SLEEP

I love resting. I love sleeping. I joke that I'm trying out for the Olympic sleeping team!

Rest and sleep are probably our most overlooked, unappreciated assets. Very simply, try to get plenty of both!

Rest is the sweet sauce of labor.
—Plutarch

TIME

There is time for everything.
—Thomas Edison

We all find time to do what we really want to do.
—William Feather

How often have you heard people say: "I don't have time!" Nonsense! Life is a matter of priorities. We all have time to do the most important things in our lives. We all eat, sleep, and go to the bathroom, our three most primal needs. Everything else follows.

You don't "have" time; you "make" time to do the things that are most important or that you most enjoy. The answer to solving the "I don't have time" fallacy is: You have to have a deadline. The reality is we meet deadlines. People get to airports on time because planes leave on time, whether or not passengers are on board.

◆ ◆ ◆

How do we maximize our time and increase our productivity so we can better enjoy our daily lives? Like most things, it's simple, but not easy. Over the past 55 years, I have heard several versions of this true story. This is the one I remember best.

Back in 1918, Charles Schwab was one of the richest men in America. He was the President of Bethlehem Steel, the largest shipbuilder and second largest steel producer in America. Schwab arranged a meeting with noted management consultant Ivy Lee and said, "Show me a way to get more things done."

Lee said, "Give me 30 minutes of your time."

Schwab asked, "How much will it cost me?"

Lee said, "Nothing . . . unless it works. Try my suggestions for three months and then send me a check for whatever you feel my advice has been worth."

Lee spent 15 minutes explaining his simple solution for maximizing time and achieving increased productivity:

- At the end of each workday, write down the ten most important things you need to accomplish tomorrow.
- Prioritize those ten items in their order of importance.
- When you arrive at work tomorrow, concentrate only on the first task. Work until it is finished. Then move onto the second task.
- Approach the rest of your list in the same way. At the end of the day, move any unfinished items to your list for the next day.
- Repeat this exact process every working day.

Lee readily admitted that it was highly unlikely that Schwab would complete his entire list. But, he said:

- You will have accomplished your most important projects.
- If you can't succeed in this manner, you can't succeed in any manner.

This Simplistic Solution to a Complex Problem (SSCP) appealed to Schwab. He and his executives tried it and found the method to be very effective. After three months, Charles Schwab sent Ivy Lee a check for $25,000. A check written in 1918 for $25,000 is the equivalent of approximately $400,000 today! Another dramatic example of a highly effective, and profitable, SSCP.

The Ivy Lee method of accomplishing business tasks meshes perfectly with the timeless philosophy that the most important things in life (health, family, etc.) should never be sacrificed or compromised for those things that are less important. Priorities! As Epictetus said, "No man is free who is not a master of himself."

◆ ◆ ◆

The old adage is: Plan your work; work your plan. It works. What separates the truly successful from the average is the way we use our time. Discipline yourself to use your time to focus on your priorities.

I am always very frustrated, and annoyed, when someone uses the excuse: "I didn't have time." What they are really saying is: "I didn't do it because it wasn't high enough on my priority list."

Think of time as an equal opportunity employer. We all have exactly the same number of minutes and hours as everyone else.

◆ ◆ ◆

To maximize everyone's time, and to make meetings more productive, all meetings should:

- Have an agenda with defined time limits for each order of business.
- Start and end on time.

It always upset me when I attended a meeting, and the leader said she was "going to wait a few minutes for the late arrivals." Why penalize those who arrived on time? We teach people what is, and what is not, acceptable behavior. By starting the meeting late, we are teaching the latecomers that it is OK to be late. No!

It's important to remember:

- Parkinson's Law: "Work expands to fill the time available for its completion."
- Everything takes more time, effort, money, and people than you think it will.
- If you want something done, give it to a busy person.
- The "to do" list far exceeds the available time. It's simply a fact of life.
- No matter how efficient you are with your time management, you never get everything done.
- Stay calm when you don't accomplish every-thing.

If a bank credited your account each morning with $86,400 but didn't carry over the balances from day-to-day and every evening canceled whatever money you didn't use that day, what would you do? Draw out every cent, of course.

Well, you have such a bank. It is called TIME. Every morning, you are credited with 86,400 seconds. Every night, you lose whatever seconds you failed to use purposefully. Each day you get a new account with 86,400 additional seconds. If you fail to use those seconds, they are lost to your forever. You can't have them tomorrow. Every day, maximize those precious seconds. Invest them to get the utmost in health, happiness, and success. Use them or lose them!

The older you get, the faster time goes. We've all heard this, but when we're young we don't understand it and/or we don't believe it. It's true. Ask anyone over 50! I asked my good friend, Prashant Ranade, why that is. He said: "It's like a roll of toilet paper . . . the closer you get to the end, the faster it goes!"

Time goes by so fast. People come in and out of our lives. Never miss the opportunity to tell them how much you love and cherish them, and how special and important they are.

Selected Thoughts on "Time"

Don't say you don't have enough time. You have exactly the same number of hours per day that were given to Helen Keller, Michelangelo, Mother Teresa, Leonardo da Vinci, Thomas Jefferson and Albert Einstein.
—H. Jackson Brown, Jr.

Many of us spend half our time wishing for things we could have if we didn't spend half our time wishing.
—Alexander Wollcott

Take time to enjoy the present.
—Alexander Reed Martin

What we love to do we find time to do.
—John Lancaster Spalding

If we take care of the moments, the years
will take care of themselves.
—Maria Edgeworth

Lost time is never found again.
—Benjamin Franklin

We have input, impact and control over how we choose to use the limited number of hours in a day. Make the best use of them.

YOUTH AND AGING

Everyone wants to get "older." No one wants to get "old." Growing older, "aging" as we now call it, is normal. We will experience health, emotional and social changes. Ideally, these changes are gradual and acceptable. As in almost all human endeavors, how we think and react to our changing circumstances is what matters. We can be positive or negative. The choices are up to us.

Selected Thoughts on Youth and Aging

Old age should be worn with pride. There
are many to whom it is denied.

Youth is not a time of life. It is a state of mind.
Nobody grows old by merely being a number of
years. People grow old mainly by deserting their

ideals and limiting their activities. Years wrinkle the skin, but giving up enthusiasm wrinkles the soul.

You can stay young indefinitely if you eat wisely, exercise, get plenty of sleep, have a positive mental outlook, and lie about your age!

We grow old as we were young.
—George Roth

You have lived a successful life if, as you grow older, the people who you hope love you actually do.
—Warren Buffett

Focus on the things over which you have Input, Impact, and Control.

CHAPTER 5
Critical Elements for Achievement

BE INDEPENDENT–DO YOUR OWN THING (DYOT)

If one advances confidently in the direction
of his own dreams and endeavors to lead the
life that he has imagined, he will meet with
a success unexpected in common hours.
—Henry David Thoreau

Do your own thing . . . what YOU enjoy, what YOU find fun and rewarding, what comes easily to YOU, what YOU are good at. What would you do for a living if you won the lottery, and in order to collect the prize money, you had to agree to work eight hours a day, five days a week?

By "doing your own thing" and being yourself, in your own genuine comfortable manner, the "real" you will become clearly apparent. As a friend once commented, "You wouldn't be concerned about what other people think of you if you realized how seldom they do!"

I follow Sophocles' motto that: "The good man is his own friend." I am basically a "loner," a person who likes, and is comfortable in, his own company. I don't aggressively try to make friends or impress people. If I make friends, great. If not, I'm fine with who I am. But I also know I don't live in a vacuum. I cannot exist totally on my own.

Work to achieve your own independence: personal, emotional, psychological, and financial. Take charge of your life. There is no need to ask permission. Choose to live the life you deserve. Never cease your pursuit of your unique individuality. Everything you need to be you, you already are. Why live anything other than the life you dream of living?

The motto of the Gestalt philosophy of psychology and the words of two of my favorite songs express my feelings about exercising our unique individualities.

The Gestalt Prayer (Fritz Perls)
I do my thing and you do your thing.
I am not in this world to live up to your expectations,
And you are not in this world to live up to mine.
You are you, and I am I,
And if by chance we find each other, it's beautiful.
If not, it can't be helped.

Words from: "Let Me Be" (The Turtles)
Please don't mistake me or try to make me
The shadow of anybody else
I ain't the him or her you think I am
I'm just trying hard to be myself . . .

Let me be, let me be
To think like I want to
Let me be, let me be
That's all I ask of you
I am what I am and that's all I ever can be.

"I Gotta Be Me" (Sammy Davis, Jr. classic)
Whether I'm right or whether I'm wrong
Whether I find a place in this world or never belong
I gotta be me, I've gotta be me
What else can I be but what I am ?
I want to live, not merely survive
And I won't give up this dream
Of life that keeps me alive
I gotta be me, I gotta be me
The dream that I see makes me what I am.
That faraway prize, a world of success
Is waiting for me if I heed the call
I won't settle down, won't settle for less
As long as there's a chance that I can have it all
I'll go it alone, that's how it must be
I can't be right for somebody else
If I'm not right for me.
I gotta be free, I gotta be free
Daring to try, to do it or die
I gotta be me.

♦ ♦ ♦

My favorite Do Your Own Thing (DYOT) example is my attitude and unique approach to golf.

My daughter-in-law, Candy Hannemann, is a golf pro, literally. She won the NCAA Division One championship, was successful on the LPGA tour for eight years, and, after coming out of an eight-year retirement, narrowly missed representing Brazil in the 2016 Olympics.

My son-in-law, Tom, is an avid, 3.3 handicap golfer who loves the game but doesn't get to play as often as he would like.

My wife, Shelly, enjoys the game, takes it seriously, practices diligently, consciously follows the rules, and has won numerous prizes in her ladies weekly "Nine Holer" events.

Me? Ned:

- Enjoys being outside and playing occasionally.
- Is not passionate about the game (can take it or leave it).
- Won't play 18 holes (nine are enough, seven would be better!).
- Can't follow the flight of the ball even when it (infrequently!) goes right down the center of the fairway.
- Frequently can't find his ball no matter where it is.
- Doesn't keep score.
- Counts only his good shots.
- Is not averse to hitting a second shot if the first one was "no good."
- Will, from time to time, move the ball to where it "was supposed to be" rather than where it mistakenly ended up.

- Sometimes adjusts the ball to an "improved lie."
- Refuses to accept any "gimme putts."
- Will stop playing when he is tired and/or sufficiently frustrated and . . .
- Given how little he practices and plays, considers himself a "pretty good golfer!"

Golf purists will cringe at my humorous, yet absolutely true, approach to golf. But my attitude and my reality is a perfect example of:

- Leading your life in your own way
- Doing Your Own Thing
- Marching to your own drummer
- Not being attached to the outcome
- Not having your eccentric or aberrant behavior negatively impact anyone else
- Exercising complete Input, Impact, and Control

Ralph Waldo Emerson said, "What I must do, is all that concerns me, not what the people think." We must accept ourselves for who we are and make the most of ourselves.

Sometimes it is more important to discover what one cannot do than what one can do. A specific example: On July 1, 2014, I made the conscious decision to discontinue my failing attempts to micromanage and "fix" the world. And what have been the results?

- My overall well-being has drastically improved. I feel dramatically better, much more relaxed and comfortable; no more stress and pressure about matters over which I had NO Input, Impact and Control. I have lifted the weight of the world from my shoulders. And . . .

- The world really hasn't noticed and doesn't care. It hasn't changed. It continues to do what it wants, when it wants and how it wants!

Selected Thoughts on Do Your Own Thing

The things that make you strange are the things that make you powerful.
—Ben Platt

Stop caring what other people think . . . Their opinion shouldn't matter more than your own.
—Stephanie Klein

Your time is limited, so don't waste it living someone else's life . . . Don't let the noise of others' opinions drown out your own inner voice. And most important, have the courage to follow your heart and your intuition. They somehow already know what you truly want to become. Everything else is secondary.
—Steve Jobs

Only a person who can live with himself can enjoy the gift of leisure.
—Henry Greber

To love what you do, and feel that it matters— how could anything be more fun?
—Katharine Graham

Permit no one to dissuade you from pursuing
the goals you set for yourselve.
—Ralph J. Bunche

To do good things in the world, first you must know
who you are and what gives meaning in your life.
—Robert Browning

Real confidence comes from knowing and accepting
yourself—your strengths and limitations—in
contrast to depending on affirmation from others.
—Judith M. Bardwick

Trust your own instinct. Your mistakes might as
well be your own, instead of someone else's.
—Billy Wilder

In all things in life, choose your conscience,
and trust your instincts and lead your lives
without regrets. It's simply easier that way.
—David Halberstam

It's a good idea to step out of line every once
in a while and look around to see if the
line is going where we want it to go.
—Earl Nightingale

When you are content to be simply yourself and don't
compare or compete, everyone will respect you.
—Lao-Tzu

This above all, to thine own self be true,
and it must follow as the night the day, you
canst not then be false to any man.
—William Shakespeare

If a man does not keep pace with his companions,
perhaps it is because he hears a different
drummer. Let him step to the music that he
hears, however measured or far away.
—Henry David Thoreau

Whoso would be a man must be a nonconformist.
—Ralph Waldo Emerson

Be yourself. Everyone else is already taken.
—Oscar Wilde

Refuse to be stampeded. Do your own thinking.
—Major Payne

As you start to walk in the way, the way appears.
—Rumi

Bloom where you are planted.
—Ruth Eleanore Rhodes

"This is my way. What is your way?
THE way doesn't exist."
—Frederich Nietzsche

What is YOUR way? Do YOUR own thing and never give up. The results will far exceed your expectations. Follow YOUR passion. YOU have the time, the input, the impact and the control to "do YOUR own thing." Practice saying: "I am comfortable being me!"

DO YOUR BEST

Every day, when we look in the mirror, hopefully we like what we see. We have little choice but to accept most of what we see because we can't change our age, our height, or the features that time has created.

But our ultimate litmus test is internal. What is most important is who we are and how we feel about ourselves. We should appreciate what we see about ourselves as human beings living on this planet: our attitude, our philosophy, our way of living, how we treat others, what we give to the community, the respect we get from other people.

If we feel good about ourselves and act accordingly, it is highly likely we will be loved, respected, and appreciated by others. For example, here are excerpts from the hand-written birthday notes my wife recently received from her daughters:

> *I am grateful for you as a human being, as a teacher, as a communicator, and a mother. I am also so beyond grateful for our relationship—how you support me, how you have been there to cheer for me, to catch me, or both, depending on the situation.*

> *You live with love, grace, and the determination to enjoy each moment and be your best self for so many. Because of you, I know how very much I'm loved.*

Reading these heartfelt words of love and admiration, what could make a mother's life more satisfying and more rewarding? These compliments and genuine words of praise and love are the ultimate rewards. Fortunately, the recipient is alive to appreciate and cherish the highest esteem in which she is held. It's like being alive to hear your own funeral eulogy!

We may think (I know I do!) that we have all the answers to almost anyone else's personal issues. I have a close friend who continuously offers his truly sage advice to his son. The advice is rarely accepted, and my friend gets very aggravated. He can't figure out why. Similarly, I frequently offer my friend my truly sage advice, which he chooses to ignore. It is easier to give than receive.

I once heard an experienced psychologist say, "People do the best they can, given who they are." Shelly Lazarus, my wife, phrased it a bit differently: "People construct their worlds to the best of their abilities so that they are comfortable in them." Those very simple thoughts have had a profound impact on me. It's amazing how often I think of those comments when I can't understand what people are thinking or doing.

Selected Thoughts on Do Your Best

If you will do each day as best you can the work which is before you, you will wake up one day and find yourself one of the competent ones of your generation.
—William James

To be yourself in a world that is constantly
trying to make you something else is
the greatest accomplishment.
—Ralph Waldo Emerson

Nobody can bring you peace but yourself.
—Ralph Waldo Emerson

Have patience, and above all, trust in yourself.

Trust who you are. Trust your instincts,
even when things don't go well.
—Billy Donovan

Ultimately, there's one investment that supersedes
all others: invest in yourself. Nobody can
take away what you've got in yourself—and
everybody has potential they haven't used yet.
—Warren Buffet

If you make a decision for the right
reasons, it is never wrong.
—Steve Kragthorpe

You don't have to be THE best. Just do YOUR best.
—Paul Hammer

ESTABLISH GOALS

What the mind of man can conceive
and believe, it can achieve.
—Napoleon Hill

Life is what we decide it's going to be. We have the input, impact, and control. We can do whatever we want. For most people, that statement is threatening. It puts the responsibility on us. We do not have much trouble achieving goals. We can do that rather easily. The problem is we do not set goals in the first place. We do not plan to fail. We just fail to plan. We never decide exactly what we want.

Scottish philosopher Thomas Carlyle wrote, "The man without a purpose is like a ship without a rudder." Setting specific goals is the basis of success. Goals are destinations that have to be reached, They are more important than the time and effort that is required to achieve them. They are dreams seen in the mind and felt in the heart that are too big to be denied. Unless you can say in one concise sentence exactly what your goal is, the chances are good that you have not clearly defined it.

Make sure your goals are realistic and suit your aptitude and personality. Then take an aggressive approach to their fulfillment. If you sit by the side of the road waiting for someone to come by and make you happy and help make you rich, it's not going to happen. Remember, the harder you work, the luckier you get!

Create your own SMART goals, ones that are:

- Specific
- Measurable
- Achievable
- Realistic
- Time bound

Selected Thoughts on Establish Goals

*You are never too old to set another
goal or to dream a new dream.*
—C.S. Lewis

If you can dream it, you can do it.
—Walt Disney

*Keep your dreams alive. Understand that to achieve
anything requires faith and belief in yourself, vision,
hard work, determination, and dedication. Remember
all things are possible for those who believe.*
—Gail Devers

*Look closely at the present you are constructing;
it should look like the future you are dreaming.*
—Alice Walker

*Beware of what you set your heart
upon. For it surely shall be yours.*
—Ralph Waldo Emerson

*No wind is favorable for the sailor who
doesn't know which direction he is going.*

*Once you make the unequivocal internal
commitment to do something, when you
absolutely know this is the time and the place to
act, the world around you will shift in all sorts of
apparently miraculous ways to make it happen.*
—Sarah Susanka

ENJOY EVERY DAY–ONE DAY AT A TIME

We have all heard those words over and over again for all our lives. But they couldn't be more true. Today is the only day we have. We have to make sure we are doing what we want to be doing and enjoying the journey.

An extremely close friend had a very unexpected stroke at the youthful age of 46. It came out of nowhere. His type of stroke is fatal 85% of the time. Miraculously, he was almost totally unaffected! I asked him what went through his mind as he was experiencing the stroke. He said, "I thought it's over and I didn't finish all I wanted to do." I imagine his reaction was common. So, before you experience a similar life-changing event, take life one day at a time and enjoy every day.

Look to this day, for it is life, the very essence of life.
In its brief course lie all the verities and realities
of your existence. The bliss of growth. The glory of
action. The splendor of beauty. For yesterday is
already a dream and tomorrow is only a vision. But
today well lived makes of every yesterday a dream of
happiness, and every tomorrow a vision of hope.
—Ancient Indian Prayer

Life is a matter of priorities. For me, it's simply "family first." If you were in a very important meeting and were interrupted and told your daughter or son had been in a serious accident, no matter how important the meeting, you would excuse yourself and tend to the situation that had instantly become most important. Your priorities had suddenly changed.

I always keep my cell phone on "just in case." Recently, I was in a meeting with an advisor. I got a call from my son, which is highly unusual in the middle of the morning. I consciously chose to take the call and politely (I hope) excused myself and spent 15 minutes on the phone with my son. The matter wasn't urgent, but it was important. In my mind, it was time extremely well spent.

Later that day I called the advisor and explained what had happened. I told him my reasoning, specifically did NOT apologize. and said that I would do exactly same thing if the situation happened again. He understood completely and said he would have done the same thing.

"Tomorrow Never Comes" (Norma Cornett Marek)

If I knew it would be the last time that I'd see you walk out
    the door,
I would give you a hug and a kiss, and call you back for
    just one more . . .
If I knew it would be the last time, I would spare an extra
    minute or two,
To stop and say I love you, instead of assuming you know
    I do . . .
Tomorrow is not promised to anyone, young or old alike,
And today may be the last chance you get to hold your
    loved one tight.
So if you're waiting for tomorrow,
    why not do it today?
For if tomorrow never comes, you'll surely regret the day

That you didn't take that extra time for a smile, a hug, or a kiss,
And you were too busy to grant someone, what turned out to be their one last wish.

Focus on the things over which you have Input, Impact, and Control.

CHAPTER 6
Topics for Personal Well-Being

LOVING YOURSELF

"Greatest Love of All" (Whitney Houston)

Everybody's searching for a hero.

People need someone to look up to.

I never found anyone who fulfilled my needs.

A lonely place to be, and so I learned to depend on me.

I decided long ago, never to walk in anyone's shadow.

If I fail, if I succeed, at least I lived as I believe.

No matter what they take from me, they can't take away
my dignity.

Because the greatest love of all is happening to me.

I found the greatest love of all inside of me.

The greatest love of all is easy to achieve.

Learning to love yourself, it is the greatest love of all.

These words exactly reflect both my feelings and experience. When we think about love, we envision classical, magical, fairy tale relationships with others. But the reality is, our first and most lasting love affair has to be with ourselves. If you cannot love and fully appreciate yourself for who and what you are, you will not be able to love others either. Give yourself permission to love yourself first, a thought over which you have significant Input, Impact, and Control.

Selected Thoughts on Loving Yourself

Have the courage to love. Since love costs nothing to give or to take, you've got nothing to lose.
—Leo Buscaglia

You are never alone when you learn how to love yourself.
—Keith Macpherson

KINDNESS

Treat everyone with whom you come in contact with the utmost kindness and respect. Treat them as the most important person on earth. Why? Because:

- It's the right thing to do and
- To them . . . they are!

Kindness should be second nature to us. It costs nothing and makes others, and us, feel great. Sometimes your simple Random Act Of Kindness (RAOK) is rewarded in ways you can't anticipate. Here's my favorite personal example.

I am a lifelong, huge Neil Diamond fan and have seen him perform countless times all over the country. In 1996, Neil taped a TV show in Nashville, Tennessee. The tickets were free, but had to be ordered in advance and picked up the morning of the taping. When I picked up the tickets at the Ryman Auditorium ticket office, the nice attendant asked me where we wanted to sit? I told her we were just excited and thrilled to be there, and it didn't matter where we sat. Any seats would be most appreciated. She gave me two tickets, and we left for a brief tour of the city and lunch.

Before entering the auditorium for the performance, I decided to tell the nice box office attendant how lovely her city was and thank her again for her cooperation. She smiled, thanked me for the compliment, and asked to see my tickets. After closely examining them, she said there had been a mistake with our tickets and gave me a different set.

Our new seats were in the FIRST row! I didn't ask for better seats . . . I just treated another human being with decency and respect. RAOK! Try it. You will feel good, and you never know what will happen!

There are other RAOK that made both the recipient and me feel much better:

A very efficient young woman was extremely helpful in scheduling my routine car service appointment. Of course, I thanked her. Then, I called her back and thanked her a second time. She was blown away: "No one has ever done that before. You made my day!"

I received a bill from my tree trimming company for their second round of service. The bill was for the same amount as the first service call. But the second time the company had an extra person on the job and worked for an extra hour. I called the owner and told him I thought he didn't charge enough. He was flabbergasted and happily agreed to accept additional compensation that he would share with his employees. I called him because it was the right thing to do. I imagine that if I ever need any special service or attention, I will likely receive it promptly.

As I was leaving my house for a 3:00 doctor's appointment, the receptionist called to tell me the doctor was running a half hour late. She suggested I get there at 3:30. I was shocked and appreciative of the most thoughtful call. Wouldn't it be nice if we were always treated with such kindness?

When people ask me what I would like for my birthday or any other special celebratory occasion, I quickly respond, "Two things: kind words and good wishes!" What greater gift could I receive?

Recently a former employee and now highly successful business executive, Margie Flynn, co-authored a book on effective leadership. In the acknowledgement, she wrote: "I will forever be indebted to Ned Grossman, who passed on numerous lessons at my first real job out of college—most notably, the importance of building lasting relationships, and the power of two simple words: 'Thank You.'"

When another former employee saw this flattering comment, she added, "Ned, you have to understand and appreciate you have impacted a lot of people!"

Both these unexpected acts of kindness and respect are lifetime highlights for me. They made me feel important, valued, worthwhile, happy, useful . . . you name it. Both of these unsolicited comments didn't take much effort, didn't cost the givers anything, and are obviously most memorable! Thank you, ladies.

◆ ◆ ◆

While it is gratifying for us to be kind to others, it is also important to be kind to ourselves. Of course we should. Why not? We deserve it! And we have complete Input, Impact, and Control over how kind we are to ourselves.

Selected Thoughts on Kindness

Be kind, for everyone you meet is fighting a hard battle.
—Plato

Everyone needs a hand to hold. Why not lend yours?

Those who are free of resentful
thoughts surely find peace.
—Buddha

No act of kindness should be considered small.
Kindness always feels good whether we are
receiving it or offering it to others. He that is
good to another is good also to himself.
—Seneca

I expect to pass through this life but once. If, therefore,
there be any kindness I can show, or any good thing I

can do to any fellow being, let me do it now and not
defer or neglect it, as I shall not pass this way again.
—William Penn

In a world that seems increasingly snarky and
judgmental, be kind. Be kind to your friends,
be kind to your family, be kind to yourselves.
And remember, just as you are, everyone
really is just doing the best they can.
—Major General Karen LeDoux

The best portion of a good man's life is his little,
nameless, unremembered acts of kindness and love.
—William Wordsworth

Sometimes we forget that one of the most precious
gifts you can give a person is an acknowledgment
of gratitude. No matter how busy you are
today, make some time to show appreciation
to someone who has touched your life.
—Mary Kay Mueller

What I want is so simple I almost can't
say it: elementary kindness.
—Barbara Kingsolver

You have not lived today until you have done
something for someone who can never repay you.
—John Bunyan

If you can learn from hard knocks, you
can also learn from soft touches.
—Carolyn Gilmore

Goodness is the only investment that never fails.
—Henry David Thoreau

*Gratitude and kindness are two of love's
most magnetic expressions, which draw to
us the highest best that life has to offer.*
—Doc Childre

*No matter what accomplishments you
make, somebody helped you.*
—Althea Gibson

*I've learned that people will forget what you
said, people will forget what you did, but people
will never forget how you made them feel.*
—Maya Angelou

Every act of kindness is an act of strength.
—Bill Russell

THINKING

If you're not in charge of your thoughts, who is?

In today's high tech world, with so much knowledge and information readily available to us, why do so many people fail to succeed? When he was asked this question, "Doctor, what's wrong with men today?" the great humanitarian and educator, Dr. Albert Schweitzer, responded, "Men simply don't think."

Why don't people think? Probably because we take our mind for granted. Since it came to us as standard equipment and was free, we do not value it or use it enough. Just a few minutes each day of deliberate thinking works wonders for our mind, for our outlook on life, and for our future happiness and success.

◆ ◆ ◆

My good friend, Howard Steindler, is a highly respected and acclaimed corporate attorney with 50 years of practical experience and innate wisdom. Early every morning he makes time to give himself "unhurried thought." He spends quiet time alone, just thinking. Sounds strange, doesn't it? He makes time to contemplate: who he is, where he is in his life, where he wants to go, how he wants to get there, what business matters need his attention, what he can do for others.

Just ten or fifteen minutes every day of highly focused reflection will have a profound positive impact on your life. Give yourself the gift of "unhurried thought." Be certain to MAKE time each day to reflect, to think and to plan. Both the tangible and intangible rewards will be disproportionate to the time and energy expended.

Several years ago I was alone in a woods. I thought to myself: What would it be like to take one hour, just one hour, and do absolutely nothing? No talking, no TV, no cell phone, no emails, no texting, no reading . . . nothing. Simply being quietly alone with myself. So, I did it.

What happened? Nothing dramatic . . . no epiphanies, nothing shocking . . . just solitude, a sense of quiet serenity, tranquility, and internal well-being. I shared this experience with my office colleagues and offered them the opportunity to do the same thing . . . take one hour by yourself . . .

come to work late, leave early, take an extra hour at lunch . . . just take one hour alone with yourself. After a month, I had heard from no one. When I brought it up again, someone said, "Oh, I could never do that. I'm way too busy." Saying you're too busy to think, to improve your mind, and to quietly enjoy your life is like saying you don't have time to stop for gas because you're too busy driving.

Most of us don't realize the enormous power of our minds and the unlimited capabilities we each possess. As William James said, "Most people live—whether physically, intellectually, or morally—in a very restricted circle of their potential being."

But simply reflecting, thinking, dreaming, and planning are not enough. You can reflect, think, dream, and plan all you want, but you also must DO! Knowledge isn't power. Applied knowledge is power. Action is required. Think action. Just Do It! (more about Just Do It in Chapter 11.) There are many talkers and few doers. Which one are you? More importantly, which will you be tomorrow and for the rest of your life?

Selected Thoughts on Thinking

Never be afraid to sit awhile and think.
—Lorraine Hansberry

All that we are is the result of what we have
thought. And all that we shall become is
the result of what we think now.
—Buddha

A man is what he thinks about all day long.
—Ralph Waldo Emerson

Change your thoughts and you change your world.
—Norman Vincent Peale

Man's mind, stretched to a new idea, never
goes back to its original dimensions.
—Oliver Wendell Holmes

Always remember, that what lies behind
you and what lies in front of you is nothing
when compared to what lies within you.
—Robin Sharma

I think recreationally, if that makes any sense,
I'll sit on the couch and three hours will go by when
I'm lost in thought. What I realized is that I'm a
visualizer. It's not meditation, and I don't do it
for any set period of time—it's just sort of been a
part of my existence, like a long standing hobby.
—Sara Blakely

We become what we think about. When we control our thoughts, we control our mind. When we control our mind, we control our lives. We have Input, Impact, and Control.

FEELINGS

As we have learned, we can control our thoughts. Often our feelings come directly from our thoughts. We can control our feelings by controlling how we think about any particular life situation. It isn't what happens to us that impacts our feelings, it's how we choose to think and react to what has happened.

◆ ◆ ◆

When a parent, friend, or relative dies, we quite naturally tend to react emotionally with sadness, tears, and grief. It's a normal human reaction. But think about this. If a close friend died and you were in a remote part of Alaska, without access to a cell phone, the internet, or any social media, you wouldn't know about the death until well after it happened. During that time, your life would go on unchanged. You would experience no sadness, no tears, no grief. But once you did get the news of this sad life event, you probably would express those innate emotions. It's not what happens to us, it's how we choose to process and react to what has happened.

When you are sad, upset, unhappy, overwhelmed, discouraged or frustrated, think positively and apply positive thoughts to your feelings about the situation. Follow Wayne Dyer's wise suggestions of how to react: "This is what has happened, and I am not going to choose negative reactions.

I am not going to choose to be immobilized and depressed. I am not going to pretend I like it. I'm just not going to allow myself to be immobilized by it. I won't. I will get through the next five minutes. Then I will get through the next five minutes, and that's how I will handle it."

TRUTH AND HONESTY

Truth and honesty are not the best policies; they are the only ones. They are absolutely essential ingredients for success. It has been said that if truth and honesty did not already exist, they should be invented as the surest way to lasting success and a happy, peaceful existence.

The simple act of telling the truth goes a long way. Nike founder Phil Knight's memoir, *Shoe Dog,* provides a classic example. His original shoe company was called Blue Ribbon. By his own admission, when the new Nike brand debuted in 1972, " . . . it was totally untested and frankly not even all that good. Yet you guys (the shoe buyers) are buying it. Why?" One buyer said, "We've been doing business with you Blue Ribbon guys for years, and we know that you guys tell the truth. Everyone else doesn't. You guys always shoot straight. So if you say this new shoe, this Nike, is worth a shot, we believe you." The rest is history. Today Nike annual sales exceed $30 billion, and their stock market capitalization is approximately $110 billion. Nike overcame their initial lack of quality by simply telling the truth.

TV commentators, newspapers, politicians, and reporters frequently assert: "The truth is . . . " Well, there is no "THE truth." "The truth" is what we think it is or what we want it to be. How do you know what "truth" to believe? I certainly don't know. Here are three examples.

An automobile accident occurs. There are four witnesses who give the police their genuinely truthful accounts of what they think happened. There are likely to be four different versions. Who's right? There is no "THE truth."

An accountant friend of mine told me, "Accountants are like artists. You give me a set of numbers, and I can paint you any picture you want." Bear this in mind when you hear or read government statistical reports. There is no "THE truth."

Several years ago I was listening to National Public Radio. There was a distinguished professor speaking on a subject about which I had absolutely no knowledge. As he spoke, I found myself nodding in agreement with his position. Then another equally distinguished professor gave an equally compelling counter opinion. Again, I found myself nodding in agreement with him. Who was "right?" I have no idea! But the incident was a great lesson in trying to form reasonable personal opinions on difficult subjects. There is no "THE truth!"

Selected Thought on Truth and Honesty

Honesty is the best policy because
it has so little competition.
—Arnold Glasgow

PEOPLE AND FRIENDS

You can get anything in life you want if you will just
help enough other people get what they want.
—Zig Ziglar

The deepest principle in human nature
is the craving to be appreciated.
—William James

Both Ziglar and James are sending the same message. Look for the good in everyone you meet. Honestly praise people at every opportunity. Tell them what they do right and genuinely compliment them. Follow these common sense suggestions, and people will treat you with the same decency and respect.

Conversely, stop being concerned about what "other people" think about you. Human nature wants us to try to please and impress others. We make that effort in many tangible ways: how we dress, where we live, how we comb our hair, what social activities we attend. All that is fine, but your success is based on who and what you are and how you treat other people, not on how you try to impress them.

It is very important to differentiate between friends and acquaintances. Friends are people we enjoy, are completely comfortable with, can talk to, and trust implicitly. Acquaintances are people we know. We all have many acquaintances but very few friends.

Loyalty is the lifeblood of real friendship. Invest deeply in a few friends, rather than superficially among many. Select your friends carefully and then stick with them.

Selected Thoughts on People and Friends

The only way to have a friend is to be one.
—Ralph Waldo Emerson

A friend is a person with whom I may be
sincere. Before him, I may think aloud.
—Ralph Waldo Emerson

The most I can do for my friend is simply be his friend.
—Henry David Thoreau

A friend is one who takes me for what I am.
—Henry David Thoreau

The better part of one's life consists of his friendships.
—Abraham Lincoln

A real friend is one who walks in when
the rest of the world walks out.
—Walter Winchell

You can make more friends in two months
by becoming interested in other people
than you can in two years by trying to
get other people interested in you.
—Dale Carneige

A friend is a present you give yourself.
—Robert Louis Stevenson

Friendship is a sheltering tree.
—Samuel Taylor Coleridge

Some people come into our lives and quickly
go. Some stay for a while, leave footprints on
our hearts, and we are never ever the same.
—Flavia Weedn

Sometimes the greatest gift you can give a friend
is your ear. Be quiet. Listen to the whole story.
Hear with your heart. You don't need to say
a word. Just being there will be enough.
—Richard Moss

Do not save your loving speeches for your friends
till they are dead. Do not write them on their
tombstones, speak them rather now instead.
—Anna Cumins

Ned, If we all treated friendships like you do,
we wouldn't have to pray for world peace.
—Jim Heck

Today make the time and the effort to tell someone just how much his or her friendship means to you.

PARENTS AND CHILDREN

Being a parent may be the world's most difficult job. It's 24/7/365. It is more complex, time-consuming, and expensive than any gainful employment. It is more complicated than anyone could imagine. The job seems to become even more daunting with each passing day.

When you reflect on your own childhood, you have your memories of what your parents did or didn't do for you.

Even if you think your parents made mistakes (and we all do!), accept the fact that they were human beings doing what they knew how to do at the time, given the unique conditions of their own lives. Can you ask anything more?

Dr. Benjamin Spock, the author of the 1960s "bible" on parenting, *Baby and Child Care*, wrote: "Love and enjoy your children for what they are, for what they look like, for what they do, and forget about the qualities that they don't have."

◆ ◆ ◆

I frequently hear parents comment that they don't give their kids "quantity" time; they give them "quality" time. You don't sit down with your child and say, "Now we're going to have quality time!" If they're young kids, they won't even understand what you're talking about. Quality time IS quantity time. One of the most precious things a parent can give to a child is a lifetime of happy memories. You never know when those magical moments will occur and how they will be remembered. Give your children lots and lots of quantity time.

◆ ◆ ◆

When my daughter Jenny was born, now 40 years ago, I "retired" from playing tennis. I had reached my level of incompetency and was a bit bored. Most fundamentally, I realized that I could always return to tennis but Jenny was only going to be an infant, a baby, and a child for a very short time. If I wanted to be a witness to, and integral part of her growing up, it was up to me to make that happen. Retiring from tennis is one of the wisest decisions I ever made.

As I wrote this, I was looking at pictures of me and my kids experiencing unforgettable times together during their now long-gone childhoods. Fabulous memories for me and, I hope, for them too. There is no amount of money that I would exchange for those moments. There is a very long list of things in life at which we have multiple opportunities. Watching your children, and now grandchildren, grow up is NOT one of them. You only get one chance at these precious moments. Don't miss them!

Children Learn What They Live

If children live with criticism,
they learn to condemn.

If children live with hostility,
they learn to fight . . .

If children live with ridicule,
they learn to feel shy . . .

If children live with shame,
they learn to feel guilty.

If children live with tolerance, they learn to be patient.

If children live with encouragement,
they learn confidence.

If children live with praise,
they learn appreciation . . .

If children live with fairness,
they learn justice.

If children live with security,
they learn to have faith in themselves
and in those around them.

If children live with approval,
they learn to like themselves.

Selected Thoughts on Parents and Children

There are only two lasting bequests we can give
our children. One is roots; the other, wings.
—Hodding Carter

Teaching kids to count is fine, but
teaching them what counts is best.
—Bob Talbert

WORRY

We all worry sometime. It's human nature. Try to minimize your worry. Generally, worry is a waste of time and energy. Worry can't do you any good and it can be very harmful emotionally, psychologically, mentally, and physically. Too many people are consumed by needless worry. They permit worry to control their actions and their lives, preventing themselves from enjoying positive, happy, productive, fulfilling, fun lives.

◆ ◆ ◆

Consider these estimates of what people worry about:

- Things that haven't happened yet and probably never will: 40%
- Things that did happen and can't be changed: 30%
- Needless concerns about your health: 12%
- Petty things that are not worth worrying about: 10%
- Legitimate matters that deserve your attention and concern: 8%

Focus your energies and time on the latter 8%, things that have not yet happened and over which you may have Input, Impact, and Control. Remember, just about all our concerns resolve themselves one way or another. Worrying does not take away tomorrow's trouble. It will only take away today's peace and drain you of today's strength. So, stop worrying. The sooner you do, the happier you'll be.

When you get in the worrying mood, try this three-step quick fix:

- Slow down.
- Relax.
- Take a deep breath.

Selected Thoughts on Worry

Finish each day and be done with it. You have done what you could. Some blunders and absurdities have

crept in; forget them as soon as you can. Tomorrow is a
new day. You shall begin it serenely and with too high
a spirit to be encumbered with your old nonsense.
—Ralph Waldo Emerson

Every problem has an opportunity for
something good. You just have to look for it.
—Kobi Yamada

As a cure for worrying, work is better than whiskey.
—Ralph Waldo Emerson

I am an old man and have known a great many
troubles, but most of them never happened!
—Mark Twain

Enjoyment of the present is denied to those
who worry too much about the future.
—William Feather

Peace of Mind: The contentment of the man who is too
busy to worry by day, and too sleepy to worry at night.
—Woodrow Wilson

Stop worrying. Put it in a pretend envelope
and throw it out the window.
—Stephanie Kite

FEAR AND FAILURE

We are all human. It is impossible to go through life without
fear, without failure, without mistakes. Everyone goes
through periods of lack of confidence and self-doubt. It is
as natural as breathing. Never fear failure. It is part of life's

pattern. Surprisingly, successful people usually make more mistakes than people who fail. But they also have more successes. They operate on the proven principle that one success can outweigh a hundred failures. Don't worry about failure. Consider the chances you miss if you don't even try. Forget your mistakes, but remember what they taught you.

Selected Thoughts on Fear and Failure

There is no question that we're going to see a few curveballs we're not used to. Sometimes we will swing and miss. There will probably be times when we feel that we have lost our swing altogether. It is these times when our greatest opportunities lie ahead of us. I have learned that failure and obstacles build character and differentiate the great people from the average. No one knows what tomorrow will bring, so don't worry about it. Goals are achieved in tiny increments. Most people quit right when they are on the verge of success. Don't let that happen to you. Failure is part of success and every successful person has failed one way or another. Accept failure and learn from it.
—Adam Grossman, Shaker Heights
High School Graduation, 1998

The only people who never fail are those who never try.
—Ilka Chase

Men who try to do something and fail are infinitely better than those who try to do nothing and succeed.
—Lloyd Jones

I cannot give you the formula for success,
but I can give you the formula for failure,
which is: Try to please everybody.
—Herbert B. Swope

Success comes in "cans;" failure comes in "can'ts."

Never let success get to your head. Never
let failure get to your heart.

Be not afraid of life. Believe that life is worth
living and your belief will help create the fact.
—William James

Those who dare to fail miserably can achieve greatly.
—John F. Kennedy

I believe that defeat is life's way of nudging you
and letting you know you're off course.
—Sara Blakely

Mistakes are the portals of discovery.
—James Joyce

LAWS OF NATURE

In your search for success and happiness, do not look for, or expect to find, undiscovered, magical miracles. Generally, they do not exist. What do exist are the absolute laws of nature. They have always been and will always be there. They are as rigid, certain, and absolute as:

- The sun rising in the East.
- Night following day.

- Spring following winter.
- Gravity.

Here are the Laws of Nature that have worked "miracles" for me:

- **Law of self-determination:** You are now and you will become what you think about.
- **Law of compensation:** As ye sow, so shall ye reap.
- **Law of accumulation:** Life is cumulative. One day at a time. No honest effort is ever lost. Every effort, small or large, accumulates and progressively grows like a snowball rolling down a hill.
- **Law of correspondence:** As within, so without. Your outer life will always be a reflection of your inner self.
- **Law of human conduct:** Let other people know they are important.
- **Law of giving:** Four of the things we crave most in life—happiness, success, peace of mind and freedom—are most easily achieved when we try to give them to others.

THE SHERI SYNDROME

Even applying all "The Laws of Nature," and all the "cause and effect" rules we've learned, life doesn't always happen as we expect, hope, or plan. Unexpected "stuff" happens. I call these unexpected events "The Sheri Syndrome."

My late wife Sheri was extremely health conscious. She didn't smoke or drink, ate right, exercised daily, got appropriate rest . . . did everything right. Then one day at age 56, she was suddenly diagnosed with pancreatic cancer. Fortunately, because she was in such good physical condition, she was able to survive the very difficult Whipple surgery and the subsequent six weeks of concurrent radiation and chemotherapy. She was tough, determined, and courageous. Most importantly, she had a fabulous attitude. Against significant odds, she lived an exemplary life for five and a half years before eventually succumbing to the cancer.

During the course of her treatments, she asked the doctors how, after having done all the right things, this sickness could have happened. Several different doctors all said the same thing: "It's just a random act."

So, in her honor and in her memory, "The Sheri Syndrome" defines unfortunate "stuff" that happens beyond anyone's control. These events aren't just medical. Other "stuff" could be not getting into the college you most want; not getting the promotion you feel you deserve; unjustifiably losing a valuable client; breaking up with a partner. The list is endless. The reality is:

- Life ain't always fair.
- "Stuff" happens!
- You can do all the right things and still suffer unfortunate outcomes.
- However, many times the "stuff" that seems tragic at the time may turn out to be fortuitous many years later. Obviously, premature death is not one of them.

*Focus on the things over which you
have Input, Impact, and Control.*

CHAPTER 7
Attributes to Cultivate

ENTHUSIASM AND PASSION

If you act enthusiastically, you will be enthusiastic. Enthusiasm, zest, and vitality are contagious. With properly directed enthusiasm, you can acquire anything you seriously want.

Selected Thoughts on
Enthusiasm and Passion

*Flaming enthusiasm, backed up by horse
sense and persistence, is the quality that
most frequently makes for success.*
—Dale Carnegie

*There is real magic in enthusiasm. It spells the
difference between mediocrity and accomplishment.*
—Norman Vincent Peale

Nothing great was ever achieved without enthusiasm.
—Ralph Waldo Emerson

If parents pass enthusiasm along to their children,
they will leave them an estate of incalculable value.
—Thomas Edison.

CREATIVITY AND IMAGINATION

We are innately blessed with a vast storehouse of both creativity and imagination. They are a part of our natural assets. It is up to us to discover, uncover, and utilize them to their maximum potential.

Selected Thoughts on Creativity and Imagination

Imagination is more important than knowledge.
—Albert Einstein

It is better to create than to be learned;
creating is the true essence of life.
—Barthold Georg

Don't let anyone rob you of your imagination,
your creativity, or your curiosity. It's your place in
the world; it's your life. Go on and do all you can
with it and make it the life you want to love.
—Mae Jemison

Instead of looking at our challenges and our
limitations as something negative or bad, we can
begin to look at them as blessings—magnificent gifts
that can be used to ignite our imaginations and help
us go further than we ever thought we could go.
—Amy Purdy

SELF-ESTEEM AND CONFIDENCE

Esteem means "to appreciate the worth of." So self-esteem means to appreciate ourselves. It is our confidence in our ability to:

- Cope with the challenges and opportunities of life.
- Trust our own mind and judgment.
- Instill in ourselves the belief and the feeling that we are worthy of happiness and success.

Your confidence is determined by how much you believe yourself to be valuable, worthwhile, important, and competent. It arises from a supreme confidence in yourself. You have to have the attitude and belief that:

- No one is better than I am.
- I can achieve whatever I set out to accomplish.
- It is impossible for me to fail.

You have Input, Impact, and Control over your own self-esteem and confidence. Earn it and use it.

Selected Thoughts on Self Esteem and Confidence

Self-trust is the first secret of success.
—Ralph Waldo Emerson

There is no feeling in the world to be compared with self-reliance—do not sacrifice that to anything else.
—John D. Rockefeller

The greatest thing in the world is to know
how to be sufficient unto oneself.
—Michel De Montaigne

Do the things that make your heart sing. Be your
own biggest fan. Bask in the glow of your potential.
Cherish yourself. Today and every day, take some 'me
time' just for you, because you're more special than
you know. Chart your own journey. See yourself as a
beautiful person because you are. Keep your hopes
shining bright. Have faith in your own wonderful self;
you really can do anything you set your mind to.
—Linda E. Knight

CHARACTER

Character is your basic being, your attitude, your standards, your ideals, what you think and feel inside. Our character is what we really are—our reputation is what others think we are.

Selected Thoughts on Character

Watch your thoughts; they become words.
Watch your words; they become actions. Watch
your actions; they become habits. Watch your
habits; they become character. Watch your
character, for it becomes your destiny.
—Frank Outlaw

*The measure of a man's real character is what he
would do if he knew he would never be found out.*
—Thomas Macaulay

COURAGE

It takes courage to acknowledge your feelings and to live honestly and truthfully in unbending accordance with those feelings. It takes courage to stick to your plan and to the unrelenting pursuit of your goal when you encounter severe obstacles.

Selected Thought on Courage

*It is easy to be ordinary, but it
takes real courage to excel.*
—Eddie Finnigan

COMMON SENSE

Common sense is a rare commodity that you either have or you don't. It's that simple. If you have to be told what common sense is, the chances are excellent you don't have it!

Selected Thoughts on Common Sense

Common sense is not so common.
—Voltaire

Common sense is seeing things as they are;
and doing things as they ought to be.
—Harriet Beecher Stowe

The three great essentials to achieve anything
worthwhile are first, hard work; second,
stick-to-itiveness; third, common sense.
—Thomas Edison

Good instincts usually tell you what to do
long before your head has figured it out.
—Michael Burke

TALKING AND LISTENING

I know that talking directly with human beings is passé. Today, emails and texts are the preferred method of communication. But I'm "old-school." Recently I thoroughly enjoyed two forty-five minute telephone conversations with good friends. The talks were personal, human, connecting, informative, fun, exciting and spiritual. Try talking with people. You might find it a rewarding experience.

We spend far too much time and energy talking and far too little time listening. Successful people tend to be good listeners. They know they will rarely make a mistake when they talk less and listen more.

Selected Thoughts on Talking and Listening

The more you say, the less people remember.
—Anatole France

All wise men share one trait in
common: the ability to listen.
—Frank Tyger

No man ever listened himself out of a job.
—Calvin Coolidge

To listen well is as powerful a means of
communication and influence as to talk well.
—John Marshall

When people talk, listen completely. I like
to listen. I have learned a great deal from
listening carefully. Most people never listen.
—Ernest Hemingway

A gossip is one who talks to you about
others; a bore is one who talks to you about
himself; and a brilliant conversationalist
is one who talks to you about yourself.
—Lisa Kirk

SMILES

Be careful! Of all the things you wear, your expression is the most important.

A SMILE costs nothing, but gives much.

It enriches those who receive without
making poorer those who give.

It takes but a moment, but the memory
of it sometimes lasts forever.

*None is so rich or mighty that he can get
along without it, and none is so poor
but that he can be made rich by it.*

*A SMILE creates happiness in the home,
fosters goodwill in business, and is
the countersign of friendship.*

*It brings rest to the weary, cheer to the
discouraged, sunshine to the sad, and it
is nature's best antidote for trouble.*

*Yet it cannot be bought, begged, borrowed,
or stolen, for it is something of no value
to anyone until it is given away.*

*Some people are too tired to give you a SMILE.
Give them one of yours, as none needs a smile
so much as he who has no more to give.*

*We don't laugh because we're happy.
We're happy because we laugh.*
—William James

PEACE, TRANQUILITY AND CONTENTMENT

*We are not human beings having a spiritual experience.
We are spiritual beings having a human experience.*
—Pierre Teilhard de Chardin

I am always attempting to be a human "being." Sometimes,
I am also a human "doing!"

Many of us are living at such a frenetic pace that true calm, stillness, and internal peace may be unknown or uncomfortable. Try spending a part of each day in "unhurried thought." You might find that there is energy and power in silence and stillness. You may become aware and appreciate the natural beauty and tranquility that surrounds you.

Selected Thoughts on Peace, Tranquility and Contentment

One of the greatest gifts you can give to yourself is a few quiet minutes each day to be 'in the moment' and feel what is in your heart. Giving yourself permission to be still and alone in your thoughts allows you to experience the power of peace.
—BlueMountain Arts

Acceptance means that you can find the serenity within yourself to 'let go' of the past with its mistakes and regrets, move into the future with a new perspective, and appreciate the opportunity to take a second chance. . . . Acceptance is the road to peace, letting go of the worst, holding onto the best, and finding the hope inside that continues throughout life.
—Regina Hill

Look for joy in small things. Life can be so busy, and we sometimes take for granted the important little things that make us smile. Stop to watch butterflies in your garden.
—Carol Schelling

*Discover the calm of solitude. Settle into
yourself, be truly alone. Welcome these times
as a gift of peace for your spirit and soul.*
—Elle Mastro

*Lean against a tree and renew your world of dreams.
. . . Laugh at your mistakes and praise yourself for
learning from them. . . . Don't be afraid to show
your emotions. Laughing and crying make you
feel better. . . . Feel calmness on a quiet sunny day
and plan what you want to accomplish in life.*
—Susan Polis Schutz

*There is no need to give up your serenity for
the sake of getting something accomplished. In
fact, accomplishment comes more surely when
your efforts are calm and your spirit is peaceful.
. . . When you're confronted with turmoil,
respond with serenity. It will lift you to a higher
level of experience and accomplishment.*
—Ralph S. Marston, Jr.

*Only a person who can live with himself
can enjoy the gift of leisure.*
—Henry Greber

Focus on the things over which you have Input, Impact, and Control.

CHAPTER 8
Your Career

WEALTH AND MONEY

Real wealth has nothing to do with the accumulation of money. Real wealth is knowledge, confidence, positive attitude and the security of knowing that no matter what happens, you can always change your thinking, your beliefs, your actions, your strategies, and still succeed.

Adopt this philosophy to ensure personal success: "You can take away my cash, my credit, all my other tangible assets that the world considers wealth. But I will always have retained the only things that really matter: my supreme self-confidence, my time, my abilities, my courage, my knowledge, my dedication, my loved ones."

Realize three ironies about money:

- The only people who "make" money work in a mint. Everyone else must earn it.

- Money is only important to the extent you don't have it.
- Money usually eludes you if you seek it directly.

There is a very simple and practical way to guarantee yourself the accumulation of money. It is so simple it is frequently overlooked. Your financial philosophy should be built on this basic premise: "Part of all I earn is mine to keep. It is mine and untouchable." To assure your financial success, participate in a forced savings and/or investment program. Payroll deduction is easy because it is automatic and works every pay period. It has been called "painless extraction" for a very good reason . . . it is! Set money aside automatically from each paycheck. Then sit back and let time and compound interest work to assure you your savings will grow.

Many people want to spend as little as possible. I "get it." But cheaper is not necessarily better. Generally, you get what you pay for. There is a huge difference between "cost" and "value."

Selected Thoughts on Wealth and Money

*The price of anything is the amount
of life you exchange for it.*
—Henry David Thoreau

We make ourselves rich by making our wants few.
—Henry David Thoreau

He is a wise man who does not grieve for the things
which he has not, but rejoices for those which he has.
—Epictetus

It's what we value, not what we
have, that makes us rich.

The real measure of your worth is how much
you'd be worth if you lost all your money.

It is good to have money and the things that
money can buy, but it's good, too, to check up
once in a while and make sure you haven't
lost the things that money can't buy.
—George Horace Lorimer

WORK AND BUSINESS

Work gives purpose, meaning, and substance to our lives. One of our greatest responsibilities—and opportunities— is to find meaningful, important work that we can perform with enthusiasm. When you find the "right fit," you will love doing it. It will fill you with joy and satisfaction and bring you all the rewards (emotional, psychological, and finan-cial) that you desire.

Thomas Carlyle said, "Blessed is he who has found his work; let him ask no other blessedness. He has a work, a life purpose." My way of emphasizing the same philosophy is by asking: What line of work would you undertake if you won the lottery and had all the money you needed, but in order to collect the prize money, you had to agree to work eight hours a day five days a week? Whatever occupation you would choose to pursue, you would undertake your work with immense passion and enthusiasm because you love it.

We all know people in jobs that may not be their first choice. These good people are reliable and trustworthy and pay the bills. To you, I give my applause and encourage you to create opportunities that better align with your passions. Continue to believe in yourself, advocate for yourself, and keep dreaming and keep working.

There is no future in any job. The future lies in the person who holds the job. What would YOU do enthusiastically eight hours a day five days a week? You enjoy Input, Impact, and Control over the answer to that very basic question. Now, Just Do It!

How to Achieve Business Success

- Enjoy what you do.
- Pretend you own the business.
- Work hard.
- Differentiate yourself.
- Arrive early. Stay late.
- Promptly return your clients' emails, phone calls, and texts.
- Get your work done on time.
- Be organized. Document (who, what, date, time).

How to Bury a Good Idea

- It will never work.
- We've never done it that way before.
- We're doing fine without it.
- We can't afford it.
- We're not ready for it.
- It's not our responsibility.

Selected Thoughts on Work and Business

*I tell journalism students that there are three
main steps to take: First, figure out what gets
your adrenaline going. Next, figure out a way
to make a career out of your passion. And
finally, outwork everyone around you.*
—Anderson Cooper

*Do your work—not just your work and no more,
but a little more for the lavishing sake: that little
more which is worth all the rest. And if you doubt
as you must and if you suffer, as you must—do
your work. Put your heart into it and the sky
will clear. And then out of your very doubt and
suffering will be born the supreme joy of life.*
— Dean Briggs

When you like your work, every day is a holiday.
—Frank Tyger

*If people knew how hard I worked to gain my
mastery, it wouldn't seem so wonderful at all.*
—Michelangelo

*You can tell when you're on the right
track. It's usually uphill.*

*Always behave like a duck. Keep calm and unruffled
on the surface, but pedal like the devil underneath.*
—Jacob M. Braude

*Everyone wants to enjoy the harvest.
Few want to do the planting.*

*Plan your work for today and every
day, then work your plan.*
—Margaret Thatcher

*The difference between a job and a
career is about 20 hours a week.*

You should not confuse your career with your life.
—Dave Barry

*All you need is the desire to succeed and
the willingness to work as long and hard
as it takes to realize your ambitions.*
—John H. McConnell

*Know yourself. Focus on using your strengths and
talents and learn how to delegate your weaknesses.*
—Toby Hynes

Genius is 1% inspiration and 99% perspiration.
—Thomas Edison

EXCELLENCE AND QUALITY

My business motto was: "Good enough isn't! Strive for perfection and settle for excellence."

Achieving excellence is not easy. It is a long, continuing process that requires commitment and significant hard work. Excellence, like success and happiness, is a journey, not a destination. It means making a decision that you are going to be the best at what you do. Commit to quality in every single detail of your work. It will make your work worth doing. This commitment to quality, this unyielding demand for excellence, will permeate you. It will give you dignity, it will give your work distinguishable character, and it will give you satisfaction.

There are no shortcuts to any place worth going.
—Beverly Sills

Excellence is not an act but a habit.
—Will Durant

The quality of a person is in direct proportion
to their commitment to excellence,
regardless of their chosen field.
—Vince Lombardi

SERVICE

Service is the key to business success. Your rewards in life are directly proportional to the service you provide others.

First comes your service; then come your rewards: personal, professional and financial.

Remember these three unfailing principles:

- Our rewards in life will match our service.
- No one can become rich without enriching others.
- Anyone who adds to prosperity will prosper in return.

You cannot stand in front of a fireplace and say, "Give me heat and then I will put in the wood." How many businesses try the illogical approach of saying, "Give us your business, then we will give you service?" The proper attitude is: "First, allow us to serve you so that we can earn your confidence and your business."

Selected Thoughts on Service

Aim for service, not success, and success will follow.
—B.C. Forbes

The rare individual who unselfishly tries to serve others has an enormous advantage. He has little competition.
—Dale Carnegie

Business is a lot like tennis—those who don't serve well end up losing.

UNCOMMON LEADERS AND PEAK PERFORMERS

The most effective leaders create a sense of esprit de corps, a group spirit that inspires others to much greater efforts and accomplishments than they would have if had they had been left on their own.

To lead people, walk behind them.
—Lao-Tzu

If your actions inspire others to dream more, learn more, do more and become more, you are a leader.
—John Quincy Adams

The most successful, highest-up executives carefully select understudies. They don't strive to do everything themselves. They train and trust others. This leaves them foot-free and mind-free with time to think. They have time to receive important callers, to pay worthwhile visits. They have time for their families.
—B.C. Forbes

Teamwork makes the dream work.
—John C. Maxwell

KNOWLEDGE AND EDUCATION

*I hear and I forget. I see and I remember.
I do and I understand.*
—Confucious

The man who does not read has no advantage
over the man who cannot read.
—Mark Twain

Give a man a fish and he will eat for a day. Teach
him how to fish and he will eat for the rest of his life.
—Chinese Proverb

Education is not the learning of facts, but
the training of the mind to think.
—Albert Einstein

Education is what remains after one has
forgotten what one has learned in school.
—Albert Einstein

Education is the most powerful weapon
you can use to change the world.
—Nelson Mandela

Education breeds confidence. Confidence
breeds hope. Hope breeds power.
—Confucius

Education is to teach men not what to
think but how to think for themselves.
—Calvin Coolidge

Knowledge is the antidote to fear.
—Ralph Waldo Emerson

An investment in knowledge always
pays the best interest.
—Benjamin Franklin

I never let my schooling interfere with my education.
—Mark Twain

LUCK

Too many people attribute the success of others to luck. Success and happiness are not matters of luck. They come from your conscious decision to make success and happiness your constant companions and to take them with you everywhere, always.

I have two favorite definitions of "luck" which have proven absolutely correct for me and many others:

- Luck is what happens when preparedness meets opportunity.
- The harder I work, the luckier I get.

Every day, do the very best you can with the certain knowledge you will start to get "lucky." You will soon discover that your luck consists of painstaking preparation and indefatigable persistence.

Selected Thoughts on Luck

Let him learn a prudence of a higher strain.
Let him learn that everything in nature, even
motes and feathers, go by law and not by
luck, and that what he sows, he reaps.
—Ralph Waldo Emerson

Among the lucky, you are the chosen.
—Chinese fortune cookie I was "lucky"
enough to receive. It's so true!

Focus on the things over which you have Input, Impact, and Control.

CHAPTER 9
Important Realities of Life

Here is my three-pronged, MOST IMPORTANT philosophy and motto:

- You are never as young or as healthy as you are today.
- No matter how much money you have, you can't buy time and you can't buy health.
- If you knew you weren't going to be here tomorrow, what would you do today?

Please read these words again, slowly. Think about them carefully. They are the foundation on which all my principles, thoughts and ideas are built. Regardless of our age, our position in life or our current state of health, these words apply to us ALL.

I first spoke those words, totally extemporaneously, when I suggested to Shelly, now my wife, that she consider retiring from her teaching position a few years earlier than she initially had planned. My work life was considerably more flexible than her more stringent teaching schedule.

These dramatic words came genuinely from my heart; they were honest, sincere, and importantly, they were absolutely and completely true. Happily, they achieved the desired effect. After much deliberation, because the idea was so novel and because she loved what she was doing, Shelly did retire early. We have lived happily ever after!

We have all heard the expression: "Life is what happens while we are making other plans." So enjoy every day! Today. Tomorrow. Every day. It's that simple. Today is the only day we have. It is up to us to enjoy it. No one can do it for us. WE have the input, impact, and control to create the life we have imagined.

PHILOSOPHIES FOR CONTENTMENT AND AN EASIER LIFE

The purpose of life is to enjoy it. The joy in life is the daily journey, not the destination. Life is cumulative; we become the sum total of our experiences. Life is too short to waste doing anything we do not really enjoy.

We are born and exist to be successful and outstanding at something. It can be challenging to think about our options. When we feel stuck, sometimes we must continue where we are while we are imagining the next steps. Our challenge is to discover our unique talents and then spend many years, and much hard work, developing them. If it were easy, everyone would be instantly successful and wealthy.

- Life is not always the way it's "supposed" to be.
- It's the way it is.

- The way we cope with life is what makes the difference.

Understand, appreciate and implement the seven "L's" of life:

- Live
- Love
- Laugh
- Lighten up
- Let go
- Listen
- Learn

ENJOYING LIFE

There are two things to aim at in life: first, to get what you want, and after that to enjoy it. Only the wisest of mankind achieve the second.
—Logan Pearsall Smith

The following two fascinating stories prove that sage adage. The first story is about a content, obscure, small town fisherman who was smart enough to follow his passion and enjoy his life every day. The second is about nine high-powered, extremely well known people who didn't enjoy their lives and suffered different fates.

Story Number One: The Fisherman

An American investment banker on vacation was at the pier in a small coastal Mexican village when a little boat with just one fisherman docked. Inside the boat were several very large tuna. The American complimented the fisherman on the quality of his fish and asked how long it took to catch them.

The Mexican replied, "Only a little while."

The American asked why he didn't stay out longer and catch more fish.

The Mexican said he had enough to support his family's immediate needs.

The American then asked, "But what do you do with the rest of your time?"

The Mexican fisherman said, "I sleep late, fish a little, play with my children, take siesta with my wife, stroll into the village each evening where I sip wine and play my guitar with my amigos. I have a full and busy life."

The American scoffed, "I am a successful MBA and can help you. You should spend more time fishing and with the additional money buy a bigger boat, and with the proceeds from the bigger boat you could buy several boats. Eventually you will have a fleet of boats. Instead of selling your catch to a middleman, you would sell directly to the processor, eventually opening your own cannery. You would control the product, processing, and distribution. You would need to leave the small coastal village and move to Mexico City, then Los Angeles, and eventually New York, where you will run your expanding enterprise."

The Mexican fisherman asked, "How long will this take?"

To which the American replied, "15 to 20 years."

"But then what?"

The American laughed and said, "That's the best part. When the time is right, you would announce an IPO (Initial Public Offering) and sell your company stock to the public and become very rich. You would make millions."

"Then what?" asked the fisherman.

The American said, "Then you would retire, move to a small coastal fishing village, sleep late, fish a little, play with your kids, take siesta with your wife, stroll to the village in the evening, sip wine and play your guitar with your amigos!"

Story Number Two: Fabled Fates, a Parable About Power

In 1923, a very important meeting was held at the Edgewater Beach Hotel in Chicago. Nine of the world's most successful financiers attended:

- The President of the largest independent steel company
- The President of the largest utility company
- The President of the largest gas company
- The greatest wheat speculator
- The President of the New York Stock Exchange
- A member of the President's cabinet
- The greatest "bear" on Wall Street
- The head of the world's greatest monopoly
- The President of the Bank of International Settlements.

Seemingly, this was a group of the world's most successful men. These were men who had found the secret of making money. Twenty-five years later, here's what had happened to these men:

- The President of the largest independent steel company, Charles Schwab, died bankrupt.
- The President of the greatest utility company, Samuel Insull, died a fugitive from justice and penniless.
- The President of the largest gas company, Howard Hobson, was in an insane asylum.
- The greatest wheat speculator, Arthur Cutten, died broke.
- The President of the New York Stock Exchange, Richard Whitney, had just been released from prison.
- The member of the President's cabinet, Albert Fall, was pardoned from prison so he could die at home.
- The greatest bear on Wall Street, Jesse Livermore, died a suicide.
- The head of the greatest monopoly, Ivan Kruger, died a suicide.
- The President of the Bank of International Settlements, Leon Frazier, died a suicide.

All of these men had learned well the art of making money, but not one of them had learned how to live!

♦ ♦ ♦

Even the smartest people can't predict the future and are frequently very wrong about their opinions. Look how wrong these famous people were:

Heavier than air flying machines are impossible.
—Lord William Kelvin, President, Royal Society, c. 1895

Everything that can be invented has been invented.
—Charles H. Duell, Director of U.S. Patent Office, 1899

Sensible and responsible women do not want to vote.
—Grover Cleveland, 1905

Babe Ruth made a big mistake
when he gave up pitching.
—Tris Speaker, 1921

There is no likelihood man can ever
tap the power of the atom.
—Robert Millikan, Nobel Prize in Physics, 1923

Who the hell wants to hear actors talk?
—Harry M. Warner, Warner Bros. Pictures, c. 1925

Selected Thoughts on Enjoying Life

Live not one's life as though one had a thousand
years, but live each day as the last.
—Marcus Aurelius Antoninus

Life is not a problem to be solved, but
a reality to be experienced.
—Soren Kierkegaard

In three words, I can sum up everything
I've learned about life: It goes on!
—Robert Frost

You've got a life to live. It's short, at best. It's a
wonderful privilege and a terrific opportunity—and
you've been equipped for it. Use your equipment. Give
it all you've got. Love your neighbor—he's having just
as much trouble as you are. Trust God and work hard.
—Norman Vincent Peale

When it's time to die, let us not discover
that we have never lived.
—Henry David Thoreau

Life is now. There was never a time when your
life was not now, nor will there ever be.
—Eckhart Tolle

An optimist gets up in the morning, goes to the
window, looks out and says: 'Good morning, God.'
A pessimist gets up in the morning, goes to the
window, looks out and says: 'Good God, morning!'

When one door closes, two doors open.

We must accept that whatever we do at any time
has the potential to anger somebody in some way.

What do we live for if it is not to make
life easier for each other.
—George Eliot

**Focus on the things over which you
have Input, Impact, and Control.**

CHAPTER 10
Family, Friends, and Mentors: *Their Wisdom and Perspectives*

Throughout my life, I have been privileged and blessed to have been the beneficiary of family, friends, and mentors who have been THE most positive influences possible. Without the time, effort, tutelage, and love of these wonderful people, I would be an entirely different, "lesser" person.

Isador Grossman, 1880-1957
My Grandfather

My grandfather, affectionately known as "Pops," graduated from Harvard College in 1902. I am thrilled to have the reflective thoughts he wrote for his class's 25th Anniversary Report in 1927. I found it particularly meaningful and impactful that his thoughts, attitudes, and experiences are similar to those of the great thinkers quoted throughout this book. I am extremely proud of his thoughtful, sensitive, and meaningful words, written 90 years ago:

A 'Class Life,' if it isn't to be a drab, prosaic catalog of events, must needs be a sort of impressionistic pen sketch. Trying to write it 25 years after graduating from college somehow sets a fellow thinking, to harking back to the dreams and ideals of his youth, and to wondering how nearly the achievements of his life have approached the goal set for himself in his college days.

He soon recognizes that, from a standpoint of purely worldly achievement, his life has fallen far short of realizing his youthful ambitions; that at best it has been a compromise with conflicting forces; and, indeed, that man may count himself reasonably successful in his career who, though he hasn't stirred the world or affected its progress as he had hoped to do in his youth, has not allowed himself to become disillusioned and crushed by the treadmill grind of the everyday; who has treated his work as a glorious adventure, full of interest, poetry and romance; who has done his daily task with zest and enthusiasm, realizing that his was but one of the amazing tasks going to make up the world's progress; who has managed in the course of his work to steal a little time for play and recreation; and who has laid aside withal sufficient competence to take care of his family and himself and his twilight days.

He soon realizes, also, as he keeps ruminating on the elements of life which most nearly make for happiness that, after all, life's greatest satisfactions do not come from, or necessarily even with, worldly or material achievement; indeed, any man may count himself happy if he and those dear to him have been blessed with reasonably good health; if he has established a home presided over by a loving, understanding, and companionable wife; if he has normal and healthy children who, while not 'eighth wonders,' are his pals and have a happy, healthy outlook on life; if he has won the affection of a few real friends, congenial spirits, who don't take life or themselves too seriously, and who are therefore comfortable and unassuming companions, taking him as he is, and for what he is, and liking him in spite of his shortcomings and weaknesses; if he appreciates spiritual things, loves beauty, and has a sympathy for his fellow beings; and if he has, because of these facts, attained a decent place in his community and the respect of his fellows.

Edward N. Grossman, Sr., 1915–1997
My Father

- *If you do a thing, do it right.*
- *If you want something done right, do it yourself.*
- *The years teach us much that the days never know.*
- *Keeping it simple is a complicated accomplishment.*
- *The older I get, the smarter my father was.*
- *We get too soon old, too late smart.*
- *Never a dull moment.*
- *Talk is cheap.*
- *Ignore (not the word he used!) all but six people and save them for pallbearers.*

When I was a kid, all our family decisions were arrived at democratically. I got one vote, my sister got one vote, my mother got one vote, and my father got four votes!

Carol H. Grossman, 1915–1992
My Mother

- *If you can't say something nice about someone, don't say anything.*
- *It's not what you say. It's how you say it.*
- *You only get one chance to make a first impression.*
- *You're better off leaving the party too soon than too late.*
- *Actions speak louder than words.*
- *If you die and go to heaven, you still have to go through Atlanta!*

When discussing visiting guests, Mom had two great lines:

- *One day a guest. Two days a pest. Three days, they smell like bad fish.*
- *All our guests make us happy . . . some by coming . . . others by leaving.*

Fred Heinlen, 1915–2010
Shaker Heights High School
Baseball Coach, 1949–1968

Fred Heinlen was referred to by Cleveland sports writers as "The Veteran Mentor." Fred was my high school baseball coach and, while I was in college, I was his assistant coach at Shaker Heights High. It was my privilege, and thrill, to assist him in 1965 when Shaker won the state championship. It was Fred's first of two state championships.

Three "Fred" incidents are particularly memorable. The first was in the spring of 1959. I was a high school sophomore. The Shaker School Board had "non-renewed" the contracts of two popular high school teachers. The students were upset and held a support demonstration in the parking lot right after school. Remember, this was 1959. Protests were unheard of then, not daily occurrences as they are today. The TV stations covered it. Many of us showed up just to see what was happening. As a result, we were late to baseball practice. If nothing else, Fred was a rigid disciplinarian and didn't tolerate any tardiness. When we eventually showed up, Fred cancelled practice, saying, "Clearly, parking lot demonstrations are more important than getting to baseball practice on time. See you tomorrow!" Lesson learned. We were never late again. There was a right way to do things: Fred's way, or no way!

Strict adherence to the rules and unrelenting discipline were the only way for Fred. In 2010, one of Fred's former football players, Jason Garrett, became the Head Coach of the Dallas Cowboys. He took over in mid-season when the Cowboys were 2-6. He immediately turned the team around. They finished 8-8. Several years later at Fred's funeral, I asked Jason how he was able to transform a losing team so quickly and so effectively. He said, "I started with the very basics that Fred Heinlen had instilled in me. I spent the first hour on the job demonstrating to my players, step by step, exactly how to put on their uniforms! As Fred taught me, no detail is too small." Well done, Fred. Your tutelage clearly lives on!

♦ ♦ ♦

When my kids were playing Little League baseball, Fred would conduct a one-hour clinic on baseball fundamentals. At the end of each clinic, Fred would tell the young players, "Please know, you are now a better baseball player than you were an hour ago." They weren't great players, but they were better players. And that's all we can hope for in life—getting better, one day at a time.

Some of Fred's sage words to savor and live by were:

- *Enjoy the day. It's the only one you've got.*
- *Ultimately, you are left with your memories, so make them good.*
- *I have no regrets. I lived the life I wanted to live.*
- *I wish you the gift of tomorrow.*
- *Blessings aplenty.*

Larry Lucchino, 1946–
Legendary Baseball Executive

A Princeton University and Yale Law School graduate, Larry was a highly successful partner at the prestigious Williams & Connolly law firm in Washington, D.C. He is the former President and CEO of the Baltimore Orioles, San Diego Padres, and Boston Red Sox. Larry pioneered the trend of building baseball-only ballparks with old-fashioned charm and smaller seating capacities. Larry has four World Series rings.

In addition to being personable, smart, dedicated, and hard-working, Larry has great common sense and a very simple approach to complicated situations. We met in 2002 when my son Adam was Larry's Red Sox intern. Adam was extremely fortunate to have Larry as a boss and a mentor and has benefitted greatly from Larry's guidance and sage advice.

As the end of Adam's three-month internship was approaching, Adam asked Larry what he should do when the internship was over. Larry's response was simply, "Keep showing up." SSCP. KISS. Fast forward 15 years. Adam is now the Chief Marketing Officer of the Red Sox!

Several years later, Adam asked Larry for advice about furthering his education. Should he go to graduate school? Business school? Law school? Again, Larry's advice was simple: "Surround yourself with good people." Adam took Larry's advice, eschewed further formal education, and now surrounds himself with 15 "good people" in the Red Sox marketing department.

These Larry Lucchino lessons are classic, real-life examples of Simplistic Solutions to Complex Problems (SSCP). His simple ideas provide clear solutions to matters over which we have Input, Impact, and Control!

Prashant Ranade, 1958–
Good Friend and Corporate Executive

Prashant is Co-Chairman of the Board of Directors of Syntel Inc. and a great leader of people. In his four years as Syntel CEO, their team grew from 9,500 to 22,000 members!

The attitudes of the people in an organization reflect the attitude of the leader. Contrary to popular thinking, you do not raise morale in an organization. Morale filters down from the top. No business can be successful without dynamic, innovative, inspiring leaders. My very close friend Prashant is a shining example. The following are excerpts from inspirational articles Prashant has written on leadership:

> *Leadership is the process of exerting social influence in order to inspire others to work collectively to accomplish a common task. Truly effective leaders are distinguished by a high degree of Emotional Intelligence, which has been found to be twice as important as technical skills and Intelligence Quotient as an ingredient of excellent performance.*
>
> *Leadership is not a title or position, but the traits within us which we must use and develop to drive success. Successful leaders are those who are able to grow and enable others to grow with them. There are five core elements to becoming the best you can be:*
>
> - *Energy and the Environment. Enthusiasm is contagious. Create an environment that inspires others to bring out the best in themselves. Set a strong team purpose. Encourage synergy and create a transparent and adaptable culture.*

- *Integrity and Trust. Integrity is key to a leader's success. Set an example and you are sure to win over your team's trust. People don't care about what you know, as long as they know that you care.*
- *Encourage Life-long, Continuous Learning. Be curious, introspective, and learn something new.*
- *Discipline and Mindset. Think big. Blend care and compassion. Be brave and take calculated risks; work hard because there are no shortcuts to success. Be positive and inspire all to pursue excellence.*
- *Self-management and Self-regulation. You will succeed by being yourself, because everyone else is already taken.*

From "The Psychology of Success Is to Have a Growth Mindset."

- *Don't make excuses for yourself. If you can fix yourself, you can fix everything else.*
- *Understand that winners never quit. There is no substitute for hard work and perseverance.*
- *Think big. Don't settle for anything less. If we can dream it, we can achieve it.*
- *Have courage. Listen to all viewpoints presented to you, but remember that the ultimate decision is yours.*
- *Own it. We succeed because of who we are, and the first step to developing a healthy, successful self-image is to take responsibility.*

- *While "working smart" is important, there is no substitute for hard work. We need to do both.*

In order to succeed, you need to know the rules of the game as well as be aware of your own abilities. Be introspective, reflect and focus on finding answers and improving, not on making excuses.

Never underestimate the power of a smile and a friendly greeting. Even if you don't know the person giving it, just smile back and greet them like they are an old friend.

Connect with people and show them compassion. Listening actively goes a long way in building long-term relationships and lifelong friends.

Shelly Lazarus, 1953–
My Wife, Retired Learning Specialist
at Hathaway Brown School

- *Be kind and gentle to yourself.*
- *Part of knowing what you want is knowing your limits. It's about boundaries, yours and others.*
- *Why do you do things? Because you can!*
- *There is no 'should.'*
- *Do what's right, be true to yourself, and don't be attached to the outcome.*
- *Celebrate people's intentions.*
- *'Next chapters' take some journeying but are worth the ride.*
- *Live today how you desire to be tomorrow. Don't just talk about it or dream it. Do it. Be it.*

- *You never know what comes from simply saying 'Hello.'*
- *Peek at what's going on, compare if you choose and then return to, or determine, your own vision of how you want to be.*

Mike Kortan, 1973–
Good Friend and World-Class Sculptor

- *My goal is to build a life from which I don't need a vacation.*
- *Never argue with fools. They will pull you down to their level and beat you with their experience.*
- *There are no mistakes in life . . . only great lessons.*
- *The farther I travel from home, the closer I am to being there.*
- *My dreams are portable. I carry them with me.*
- *Many hands make light work.*
- *Life's truths don't match our feelings.*

Margie Flynn, 1959–
Corporate Executive

Margie Flynn is the co-founder and Principal of BrownFlynn, a highly successful corporate sustainability and governance consulting firm in Cleveland, Ohio. She co-authored an inspirational book on leadership, *Uplifting Leaders* (*Who Happen To Be Women*). I was Margie's first boss after she finished college.

Margie's basic philosophies emphasize exactly what her book embodies:

Life has a funny way of complicating simple things. Because books, courses, lectures, seminars . . . they usually go into deep descriptions about the profound qualities needed to be a good leader. But when you break it down, the basic requirements are the same ones we learned as children:

- *Always be yourself.*
- *Do the right thing.*
- *Stay curious.*
- *Be honest and positive.*
- *Trust your inner voice.*

Her favorite rules to live by include:

- *Remember the power of "thank you" and a smile.*
- *Don't take yourself too seriously.*
- *Take time to celebrate.*
- *Failure is not the worst thing that can happen. Not trying is.*
- *Make time for others without expecting anything in return.*
- *Never forget your roots; they keep you grounded.*

Keith Macpherson, 1978-
Spiritualist

Keith Macpherson is a friend, and inspiring yoga and mindfulness teacher in Winnipeg, Canada. As you read his philosophies, realize how this young up-and-coming spiritual leader's ideas and thoughts so closely mirror those of his legendary predecessors.

- *You can't control the behavior of those around you, but you can control how you choose to respond.*
- *There are some things in this world that you just can't change. But one thing you can change is the way you choose to look at things.*
- *Is the current thought you are thinking in alignment with how you want your life to be? If not, you can change it right now.*
- *There are no limits to what lies ahead of you. You will accomplish great things when you believe in the unlimited potential that exists within you.*
- *Allow yourself to feel your feelings. They are an authentic part of who you are.*
- *Today is the perfect time to let someone know that you love them.*
- *If you are being hard on yourself, it is time to stop beating yourself up and begin loving who you are.*
- *Simplify your life and you will gain the clarity you have been seeking.*
- *What is the one step you will take today to lead you closer to your dream?*
- *Rushing through your life is a waste of energy. Slow down and experience each step of your journey.*
- *May I be a blessing to all those who cross my path today.*

- *If you are truly present in this moment, you can consciously choose how you want to feel right now.*
- *Give up the need to control the behavior of those around you. You are only responsible for your own self.*
- *You are loved for exactly who you are. You no longer have to try to be something you are not.*
- *Instead of being overwhelmed by all there is to do, focus your attention on one thing at a time.*
- *Practice giving today with no expectations of receiving anything in return.*
- *Let your intuition guide you today. Your initial 'gut feelings' are always the right path to follow.*
- *Practice loving others for exactly who they are, not for what you want them to be.*
- *Practice listening at a deeper level today. Is it possible to just listen without feeling the need to interrupt?*
- *One of the most generous gifts you can offer someone is that of your full attention. Listen more than you speak today.*
- *Think only those thoughts and speak only those words that complement how you want your life to be. You are always creating your own reality.*
- *We are only here for a short time. Be sure that you are daring to live the life you have been imagining for yourself. Your life is now!*
- *Take a deep breath and realize that in this moment you are present. Then decide what you want to intentionally focus on, one step at a time.*

- *Stop worrying about what others will think and commit to acting on the truth that is whispering in your heart.*
- *Our capacity to love others is directly proportional to the amount that we can love ourselves.*
- *Allow the day to unfold one moment at a time. When you stay present to each moment unfolding, you no longer are worrying about the future or second-guessing the past.*
- *Listen to the inner whispers of Spirit within you. This is where the magic is.*
- *Take time to be silent and listen. From the stillness come the answers.*

Focus on the things over which you have Input, Impact, and Control.

CHAPTER 11
Simple Philosophies to Live by

KEEP IT SHORT AND SIMPLE (KISS)

The KISS principle originally stood for "Keep It Simple, Stupid." In today's politically correct society, it stands for "Keep It Short and Sweet" or "Keep It Short and Simple." Whatever your preference, the point is: Keep It Simple.

Set, and keep, simple-to-understand, easy-to-accomplish goals. Simplicity means keeping first things first and not losing sight of our focus, of what is important. When things get complicated, life feels overwhelming and out of control. When that happens, immediately revert to the KISS principle. Remember Confucius's philosophy: "Life is really simple; but we insist on making it complicated."

I aggressively try to practice the KISS principle. I know very little about automobiles, electronics, technology, and mechanics. For instance, when I'm driving my car I know two things:

- When I'm in "D," I go forward.
- When I'm in "R," I go backward.

I have no idea how that happens, but it does. That's all I need to know to get me from point A to point B. The details would only give me a case of a disease I call "mental indigestion."

Two KISS examples come to mind from my personal medical history:

When I was 22, I broke my ankle sliding into second base, had major surgery, and was in a cast for four months. When the cast was removed, I asked my surgeon what physical activities I could do. His answer? "You can do anything you want and when it hurts . . . you'll stop!"

Forty-some years later, the ankle had become permanently swollen and began to cause some slight pain and discomfort. I consulted my internist for his expert opinion. After a careful examination, he suggested two options:

- Go to an orthopedic surgeon for further evaluation or
- Don't tie your shoelaces so tight!

Guess which option I chose. Now, years later, with slightly looser-fitting shoes, any pain and discomfort are completely gone!

With all the complexities of today's modern medicine, KISS worked both times. And I exercised complete Input, Impact, and Control.

◆ ◆ ◆

In the broader world, the election of our last two Presidents is another prime example of the impact and effectiveness of the KISS principle. Both Democrat Obama and Republican Trump promised voters "hope" and "change." They each used their unique personalities and charisma to sell themselves. Their political platforms had far less to do with their victories than did their very simple, and well orchestrated, promises of "hope" and "change."

Selected Thoughts on KISS

You can't steal second base and keep one foot on first.
—Frederick B. Wilson

You can observe a lot by just watching.
—Yogi Berra

If you can't explain what you're doing in simple English, you are probably doing something wrong.
—Alfred Kahn

The obvious is that which is never seen until someone expresses it simply.
—Khalil Gibran

*Simplicity is making the journey of this
life with just enough baggage.*
—Charles Dudley Warner

*Knowledge is the process of piling up facts;
wisdom lies in their simplification.*
—Martin H. Fischer

JUST DO IT!

The iconic "Just Do It" Nike slogan:

- Is absolutely true.
- Is the quintessential example of the KISS principle.
- Has been my personal motto for years.
- Is on my car license plate.

How do you do anything? You "just do it!" Here are a few examples. Years ago, I decided that soda pop wasn't good for me and I would eliminate it from my diet. So what did I do? I just stopped drinking soda pop. That's a very Simplistic Solution to a Complex Problem (SSCP). But how else do you do it? You don't need a psychologist's recommendation. You don't need anybody else's approval. You either drink soda pop or you don't. Those are the only two options. The decision is up to you. And, happily, you can implement your decision immediately. There are no excuses!

The same "Just Do It" philosophy applies to all nutritional intake. An easy way to not eat "junk food" is to not have unhealthy foods in the house. If there is no ice cream, no candy, no cookies, you can't eat them. You didn't become overweight overnight. You won't lose excess weight in one day either. Like everything in life, our actions, our successes are "one day at a time." The results will be cumulative. Be patient with yourself. Eat right . . . one day at a time. Another Just Do It, Simplistic Solution to a Complex Problem (SSCP). Try it. This simple formula will work!

Wayne Dyer told this story about a new patient who came to him. She was an habitual "nail biter," whose fingers were bloody stubs. She had spent years seeking help from friends, psychologists, psychiatrists, and others. She was willing to "do anything" to rid herself of this lifelong, embarrassing, frustrating addiction. Wayne said he could help her and suggested she should come back the next week for another session. She was thrilled and reiterated that she would "do anything" to stop biting her nails. He said there was one thing she had to do during the next week . . . "don't put your fingers in your mouth!" KISS.

She said, "You know, no one has ever explained it to me quite that way!" If you want to stop biting your nails, there is only one way: don't put your fingers in your mouth! KISS.

How do we accomplish those goals? One minute at a time. Then another minute. We say to ourselves, "I can get through the next minute without putting my fingers in my mouth. Then I can go another minute." The minutes become hours, the hours become days. One day at a time! The only way.

♦ ♦ ♦

Those were tangible, physical examples. How about a mental example? Try this. Close your eyes and picture a long-stem red rose sitting in a slim, beautiful vase. Now think about a giraffe walking through a forest eating leaves off tall treetops. How did you do that? How did your mind go from thinking about a beautiful rose to immediately thinking about a tall, hungry giraffe? I certainly don't know. And I doubt anyone can tell you simply. You Just Did It!

Selected Thoughts on Just Do It

A successful person is one who went ahead and did the things the rest of us never quite got around to.
—Fortune Cookie

The most effective way to do it, is to do it.
—Amelia Earhart

All the good maxims have been written. It only remains to put them into practice.
—Blaise Pascal

Action expresses priorities.
—Mahatma Gandhi

You don't have to see the whole staircase, just take the first step.
—Dr. Martin Luther King, Jr.

Action may not always bring happiness; but there is no happiness without action.
—Benjamin Disraeli

Life is too deep for words, so don't
try to describe it, just live it.
—C.S. Lewis

What must be done eventually
should be done immediately.
—Jeremy Foley

How wonderful it is that nobody need wait a single
moment before starting to improve the world.
—Anne Frank

There is more comfort in doing what you
can than getting done nothing at all.

Without action, the best intentions in the world
are nothing more than that: intentions.
—Jordan Belfort

Well begun is half done.
—Aristotle

Whatever you can do, or dream you can, begin
it. Boldness has genius, power and magic in it.
—Johann Wolfgang Von Goethe

The matzoh reminds us that when the chance
for liberation comes, we must seize it, even if
we do not feel ready—indeed, if we wait until
we feel truly ready, we may never act at all.
—Velveteen Rabbi Blog

How To Get Things Done?—Just Do It!

SIMPLISTIC SOLUTIONS TO COMPLEX PROBLEMS

It was Super Bowl Sunday, 2017. I got up, looked out the window, perused the newspaper, and saw a bit of the Sunday morning news and interview shows. I quickly found:

- It was cloudy, gray, and foggy outside. (I wanted it to be sunny!)
- There was unending talk about who would win the Super Bowl.
- There was both overbuilding and terrible traffic in town.
- The political parties were fighting.
- The courts and the politicians disagreed.
- The moral fiber of America was being questioned.
- There were unlimited negative, debilitating stories!

Even though it was early in the day, I was already fatigued and a bit demoralized over my perceived state of the world. I was tired of all the talk. So . . . I decided to focus on the things over which I had Input, Impact, and Control. I put on my exercise clothes, walked out the door, and did my normal, daily 3.5 mile walk/run.

Fifty-six minutes and twenty-eight seconds later, after a very enjoyable energizing workout, I was back at my desk. And the very big outside world hadn't changed. (Although the sun had come out and the sky was clear and blue . . . honestly!)

- There was still unending talk about who would win the Super Bowl.
- There was still overbuilding and terrible traffic in town.
- The political parties were still fighting.
- The courts and the politicians still disagreed.
- The moral fiber of America was still being questioned.
- There were still unlimited, negative, debilitating stories!

But my small personal world had changed . . . significantly. I was no longer psychologically fatigued or demoralized. I felt great . . . physically, mentally, emotionally, and psychologically—all because I had done the most important life activities that no one else could do for me. I had been mentally and physically active.

- I prioritized my life and did the most important things in my world . . . taking good, appropriate care of my most important assets—my mind and my body.
- I hadn't just talked the game. I had "walked the walk" and had "run the run."
- I "Just Did It."

ALL my bromides had held true:

- Simplistic solutions to complex problems? Yes!
- Focus on the things over which you have input, impact, and control. Yes!
- Just do it! Yes!

You've heard all these many times before. Try them. You'll like them! Is there any other way? What's the downside?

SURROUND YOURSELF WITH GOOD PEOPLE

I owned a small, independent employee benefits consulting firm. After a 45-year career, I sold the business to a large, international, publicly traded insurance organization. I was very fortunate to have wonderful savvy and experienced accountants and lawyers. Everything went as smoothly as could possibly have been expected. In spite of that ease, there were four different documents executed (one was 59 pages!). I learned many things in the process. The two most important were:

- I could never have read and understood the documents by myself. I probably knew the meaning of each individual word, but not what they meant collectively from a legal standpoint.

- The essence of legal agreements is not found in what is written in the documents, but in what is omitted!

Suffice it to say, I was very pleased to have surrounded myself with the sage advice of good friends and good people. Thank you, Howard, Allan, and Les!

♦ ♦ ♦

As is clearly evident, it is most advantageous, and probably essential, to "surround yourself with good people." What happens when you don't? Here are two examples:

I have a long-time friend who is sweet, kind, very hard-working, overly trusting, and not particularly business savvy. Within a few years, she made two poor important choices because she did not seek appropriate professional advice before making significant decisions:

- She got "ripped off" when she sent a large sum of money to California as a deposit on a car that was supposed to be delivered to her in Cleveland. She never heard from the "seller" and lost all her money.
- She obtained a "do-it-yourself" divorce from her husband, who had convinced her she did not need a lawyer. She ended up agreeing to receive no alimony and no child support for her two children.

Had she taken the time to consult with friends and/or mentors and/or trained, experienced professional advisors, she probably would have made other, more beneficial decisions. Let me emphatically restate the obvious: "Because you don't know what you don't know, surround yourself with good people."

You might say, "Perhaps, she couldn't afford professional advice." That's a logical possibility, but my thought is she probably lost more money by not "surrounding herself with good people" than the appropriate professional advice would have cost.

◆ ◆ ◆

No matter what your profession, it's almost impossible to know enough to do everything by yourself. There's just too much information, too much to do, and too little time. We have to "surround ourselves with good people" (experts) who can help make our lives "as easy as possible." If you can afford to pay people to do it for you, hire others to do the things you don't like doing. Focus your time and efforts on the things in life you love, enjoy, and do well. Work hard to earn enough money so you don't have to do what you don't like to do or don't know how to do. Surround yourself with good people!

Focus on the things over which you have Input, Impact, and Control.

CHAPTER 12
Death and Dying

Death and dying are obviously very "touchy" subjects. Intellectually, we all know death is inevitable, although many of us don't want to think about it (if we don't think about it . . . it won't happen!?!?) and/or admit it and/or talk about it and/or properly prepare for it. Eventually, sooner or later, we will all face these issues, for ourselves and for our loved ones. It is NOT a matter of "if." The practical, unanswerable questions are: When? Where? How? Why?

ARE YOU PREPARED?

When your time does arrive, will you prepared? Emotionally? Psychologically? Financially? Legally? Start thinking about it NOW. It doesn't matter how old you are or the state of your current mental or physical condition. Talk with your family and friends, NOW. NOT talking about it and NOT preparing for it will NOT prevent your inevitable demise. Guaranteed! Breaking News: The death rate is holding steady at 100%.

♦ ♦ ♦

Death isn't the real problem. It's the process of dying. The question we need to answer is how much "input, impact, and control" do we choose to exercise during the dying process. Are we going to be:

- "Active" and address the inevitable head on and prepare accordingly, or
- "Passive" and choose to ignore the inevitable and not consider actions and decisions?

There is no right or wrong answer. It's a matter of clearly considering the subject, evaluating the alternative courses of action, and making conscious, informed decisions.

The Conversation Project is an organization dedicated to helping people talk about their wishes for end-of-life care. They site statistics:

- 90% of people say that talking with their loved ones about end-of-life care is important. 27% have actually done so.
- 82% of people say it's important to put their wishes in writing. 23% have actually done so.

As with many life decisions, "doing nothing" is in reality deciding "not to decide." And that's perfectly acceptable. But it is critical to realize:

- It is NOT: "I can't decide."

- It is: "I am deciding not to decide. I choose not to deal with this matter at the present time."

Over the years, I have made dying and death frequent topics of conversation with family and friends. A wide variety of thoughts, opinions, and emotions have been expressed. When I specifically ask people, if they had a choice, how they would prefer to die, they invariably say:

- Just not wake up one day.
- Simply drop dead.
- Have a short, painless terminal illness.

Most dramatically, not one person has ever expressed a desire to:

- Outlive their usefulness.
- Exist with a very poor quality of life.
- Be a burden to their family and friends.
- Be kept alive by artificial means.

There are myriad issues and options about this highly personal topic. You can go online and find unlimited information, terms, definitions, statistics, and options that will be helpful in the decision-making process. It can be mind boggling. For example, a very basic decision is whether or not to have a will. I have been told that if you die without a properly executed will:

- Your assets may not go where you wanted them to go and
- Settling your estate may be more expensive than it needs to be.

RELEVANT PERSPECTIVES

There are countless articles about end-of-life issues. Here are two perspectives from experienced and respected physician experts.

Ira Byock is a palliative care physician. His article "Dying Shouldn't Be So Brutal" appeared in the February 1, 2015 *New York Times.* His thoughts included:

Most Americans don't want to think about dying.

Life is precious and worth fighting for, so every option is worth considering. But modern medicine has yet to make even one person immortal. Therefore, at some point, more treatment does not equal better care.

People who are approaching the end of life deserve the security of confident, skillful attention to their physical comfort, emotional well-being, and sense of personal dignity. Their families deserve respect, communication, and support.

Most people want to drift gently from life, optimally at home, surrounded by people they love.

An American living with cancer has a roughly one in four chance of dying in a hospital and a

*similar chance of spending a portion of his or
her last month in intensive care. The chances are
higher with chronic lung or heart disease.*

*Less than 45 percent of dying Americans receive
hospice care at home, and nearly half of those
are referred to hospice within just two weeks of
death. Hospice was designed to provide end-
of-life care, but this is brink-of-death care.*

Jessica Nutik Ziller, a doctor practicing both critical and palliative medicine in Oakland, California, has written *Extreme
Measures: Finding a Better Path to the End of Life.* In a fascinating *New York Times* article, February 18, 2017, her
thoughts included:

*Too many of our patients die in overmedicalized
conditions, where treatments and technologies are
used by default, even when they are unlikely to help.*

*By the time patients are approaching the end, they are
often too weak or disabled to express their preferences,
if those preferences were ever considered at all.
Patients aren't getting what they say they want. For
example, 80 percent of Americans would prefer to
die at home, but only 20 percent achieve that wish.*

*We need to learn how to make a place for death in
our lives, and we also need to learn how to plan for
it . . . when patients are prepared, they die better . . .
what people want when it comes to end-of-life care
is almost never as much as what we give them.*

◆ ◆ ◆

My sister Joan is 73. She just revised her estate plan and end-of-life wishes. Her documents are organized, simple, and concise. They clearly spell out her exact wishes under almost any conceivable circumstances. They contain her will, trust, durable power of attorney, health care surrogate, and living will. She has put her own mind at ease and made it very easy for her survivors to execute her desires. Nice going, Joan!

It is important to understand, and accept, the indisputable fact that after our loved ones depart, "Life Goes On." Our issue is how we deal with these very sad, traumatic situations. The choices are obvious:

- We reluctantly accept the realities of death and consciously soon choose to "move on" with a positive attitude, not forgetting, but living, the life we are privileged to have, or

- We focus on our loss and what was and prolong our own sadness and difficulties with a negative attitude.

It is highly ironic that I am writing these words on the anniversary of my late wife Sheri's passing! I believe in synchronicities, not coincidences, so it is very important to relate my personal observations, thoughts, and feelings on this memorable day.

Sheri was the most popular person I have ever known. She was universally loved, respected, and revered by everyone she met. Even now, nine years after her death, someone recently commented, "You couldn't meet Sheri and not like her."

Her funeral was attended by over 700 people, who literally came from all over the world! It has hit me very dramatically that today I have received less than half a dozen calls, emails, or texts remembering Sheri, acknowledging this special day and its meaning. I imagine that most people have forgotten the date, and many who do remember are, for their own appropriate reasons, uncomfortable bringing it up.

We must accept that after we're "gone," "not living at the present time," have "passed," "crossed over," "left our bodies," "died," or however you choose to phrase it, life goes on. So as we move forward on life's highly uncertain path, please make time today to live, love, and laugh. Realize and appreciate that all good things come to an end. Life will too. How are you preparing to deal with the inevitable? When thinking about these most difficult topics, you might consider that your decisions are not just about YOU. They are also about helping your loved ones at a time when they are most emotional, stressed, and vulnerable.

The question is frequently asked, "Are you afraid of dying?" A logical, realistic question. Equally logical and realistic is the infrequently asked question, "Are you afraid of living?" The inference being: Are you afraid to live "too long"?

SPECIFIC END-OF-LIFE EXAMPLES

With today's medically enhanced technology and focus on wellness and overall healthy lifestyles, our life expectancies have increased dramatically. Today many people may be living longer than they want to live! Here are three examples:

- I saw a friend I hadn't seen in several years. I asked him how things were going. He said, "Great, except for my Dad. He's 93 and all he wants to do is die. But, I told him, 'Dad, we're not going to let you die!'" I thought: "Really?!? You must have unique powers I don't know about . . . not "letting" your father die!" That conversation was about seven years ago. I wonder what has transpired with his Dad since?!?

- My in-laws were married for 72 years. Their end-of-life experiences represent very opposite ends of the "Death and Dying" spectrum. At age 92, Harry had a heart attack on Thursday and died on Friday. Fanny continued to live what to her was a very unhappy existence. She sold her house and resided in two assisted living facilities. We visited her shortly before she passed away at 95. Before we left, we asked her if there was anything we could get her. She said, "Yes! Poison!"

- My wife has an aunt who is 103(!). She has lived in her own apartment, with appropriate care and assistance. She recently fell, broke her leg, and is now in a nursing home, knowing her cherished apartment is being closed. At our last visit, she told us, "It's enough. I'm tired. I don't want any more birthdays. Every night when I go to sleep, I pray I won't wake up!"

We have all heard these stories. The question we have to ask ourselves is, "What am I going to do to prepare myself for the inevitable?"

Chapter 50 of the *Tao Te Ching* (translated by Stephen Mitchell) offers an interesting perspective on death:

> *The master gives himself up*
> *to whatever the moment brings.*
> *He knows that he's going to die,*
> *and he has nothing left to hold onto;*
> *No illusions in his mind,*
> *no resistances in his body.*
> *He doesn't think about his actions;*
> *they flow from the core of his being.*
> *He holds nothing back from life;*
> *therefore he is ready for death,*
> *as a man is ready for sleep*
> *after a good day's work.*

♦ ♦ ♦

With the inevitability of death in mind, fully enjoy your life, NOW:

- When you can.
- While you can.
- Because you can.

Give yourself your own parties. Actively celebrate and commemorate happy, euphoric days, events, and memories: birthdays, weddings, holidays, family and friends.

♦ ♦ ♦

My mother had a great expression: "You're better off leaving the party too soon than too late." She was referring to social gatherings, but this wisdom can be applied aptly to even more important life situations: your working career and life itself.

♦ ♦ ♦

As "the end" eventually approaches, I hope you will have lived life fully and be in a position to appreciate fully the words of Paul Anka's classic song made famous by Frank Sinatra: "My Way."

> And now the end is near;
> And so I face the final curtain.
> My friend, I'll say it clear,
> I'll state my case, of which I'm certain.
> I've lived a life that's full.
> I've traveled each and every highway;
> And more, much more than this,
> I did it my way.
> Regrets, I've had a few;
> But then again too few to mention.
> I did what I had to do,
> I planned each charted course;
> each careful step along the byway,
> and more, much more than this,

166

I did it my way.

Yes, there were times, I'm sure you knew

When I bit off more than I could chew.

But through it all, when there was doubt,

I ate it up and spit it out.

I faced it all and I stood tall;

and did it my way.

I've loved, I've laughed and cried.

I had my fill; my share of losing.

and now, as tears subside,

I find it all so amusing.

To think I did all that;

and may I say—not in the shy way,

Oh no, oh no, not me,

I did it my way.

For what is a man, what has he got?

If not himself, then he has naught.

To say the things he truly feels;

and not the words of one who kneels.

The record shows I took the blows—

and did it my way!

Selected Thoughts on Death and Dying

Even death is not to be feared by
one who has lived wisely.
—Buddha

Don't die with your music still in you.
—Wayne Dyer

*As a well-spent day brings happy sleep, so
a life well spent brings happy death.*
—Leonardo da Vinci

*Once you are ready to die, you do not
suffer so badly from the horror.*
—Chris Cleave, *Little Bee*

*In corporate America, when someone
dies, three things happen: they praise you;
they bury you; they replace you.*
—Dennis R. Knight

*Be happy while you're living for
you're a long time dead!*
—Scottish Proverb

*I would rather die a meaningful death
than to live a meaningless life.*
—Corazon Aquino

I would rather die of passion than of boredom.
—Emile Zola

*When you were born, you cried and the
world rejoiced. Live your life so that when
you die, the world cries and you rejoice.*
—Cherokee Saying

*You've gotta know when to hold
'em, know when to fold 'em.*
—Kenny Rogers

The last suit you wear won't need no pockets.
—Larry Williams, Larry Shell, Kim Williams

No soul remembered is ever really gone.
—Mitch Albom

It's important to put the idea of dying in your daily life because it helps you to appreciate your existence on this planet. Death can come at any second and change everything. It can be the death of a loved one or your own. People spend endless time on total insanity, thinking that they will be here forever. Life is temporary. Make every day meaningful and don't spend time on bullshit.
—Marina Abramovic

The departed, whom we now remember, have entered into the peace of eternal life. They still live on earth in the acts of goodness they performed and in the hearts of those who cherish their memory. May the beauty of their life abide among us as a loving benediction.
—Ancient Jewish prayer

The bitterest tears shed over graves are for words left unsaid and deeds left undone.
—Harriet Beecher Stowe

Focus on the things over which you have Input, Impact, and Control.

CHAPTER 13
Words to Live By

You have heard many of these very simple pearls of wisdom before. Some are my own creation; others aren't. I can't provide attribution for them all. My apologies, and thanks, where there is no attribution. From wherever they came, enjoy them . . .

Smile BE BALANCE

Believe

Relax Live ENJOY

LOVE LISTEN Laugh

Celebrate

EXERCISE

PRIORITIZE PEACE

QUIET Think DREAM

LET GO   BE YOURSELF

BE KIND   BE FLEXIBLE

Don't worry

Calm down   BE HUMBLE

HAVE FUN

EAT HEALTHY   WORK HARD

Drink water   Be open

SCHEDULE DOWNTIME

HAVE BOUNDARIES   BE CONSISTENT

WHAT'S NEXT?   *Establish limits*

LET IT UNFOLD Life goes on

ENJOY EVERY DAY

TRUST YOUR INSTINCTS LIFE IS CUMULATIVE

ENOUGH IS ENOUGH

DO IT NOW Less is more

Never give up KEEP IT SIMPLE

YOU HAVE TIME CONTROL YOUR ENVIRONMENT

Perception is reality Have realistic expectations

GIVE YOURSELF PERMISSION

FOLLOW YOUR PASSION SAY "THANK YOU."

LISTEN. THINK. DECIDE. MAXIMIZE YOUR POTENTIAL

What's the downside? **CREATE SMALL SUCCESSES**

TAKE A DEEP BREATH **DO YOUR OWN THING**

Go with the Flow

DO THE RIGHT THING

Make your own choices **LIVE IN THE MOMENT**

What am I doing? YOU CANNOT BUY TIME

SHOULDA, COULDA, WOULDA, IF

Change is inherently stressful

IF NOT NOW, WHEN?

You cannot buy health

SAYINGS I DIDN'T KNOW
WHERE ELSE TO PUT!

The most stressful situations are the unresolved.

People with humility are secure.

*Experience is what you get when you
don't get what you want.*

*The longer it takes for something
to happen, the less likely it will.*

You act in haste, repent in leisure.

A 'no' answer is better than no answer.

*Everything takes more time, effort,
money, and people than you think.*

*You get treated in life the way you
teach people to treat you.*

The most respected people tell it like it is.

We have the faults of our virtues.

The urgent drives out the important.

A bad idea is better than no idea.

People mean well. They just aren't smart.

Rich or poor, it's good to have money.

You are what you eat.

*Accept insults as compliments from
people who don't know any better.*

*Accept people as they are. Do not try to
make them how you want them to be.*

Lead your life in your own way.

Life is subject to change.

You don't have to be smart. Just don't be stupid.

There are no ordinary moments.

*Know who you are. Know what you
can do. Know what you can't do.*

You can talk the game, but can you play the game?

No test measures common sense and basic decency.

*One of the secrets of a happy life is
continuous small treats.*

Focus on being productive instead of being busy.

Err on the side of generosity.

When your cup is full, stop pouring.

If it's to be, it's up to me.

Detours don't have to be dead ends.

If you have an itch, scratch it.

Play in your own sandbox.

The best gifts are tied with heartstrings.

What you focus on expands.

Rewards are usually anti-climactic—
the fun is in the doing.

Don't bet against Mother Nature or Father
Time. They're both undefeated.

How little we realize what power we have
to lift and change someone by saying, "You
are really important. You count."

Don't dream of thousands of reasons why you can't
do what you want to; find one reason why you can!

The only way to keep the goodwill and high esteem
of the people you work with is to deserve it. Each
of us, eventually, is recognized for exactly what
we are—not what we try to appear to be.

What the superior man seeks is in himself;
but what the small man seeks is in others.
—Confucius

Nothing is so fatiguing as the eternal
hanging on of an uncompleted task.
—William James.

Experience is not what happens to you; it's
what you do with what happens to you.
—Aldous Huxley

Sincerity is the foundation of the spiritual life.
—Albert Schweitzer

*Real confidence comes from knowing and accepting
yourself, your strengths, and your limitations—in
contrast to depending on affirmation from others.*
—Judith M. Bardwick

*The most exhausting thing in life, I have
discovered, is being insincere. That is why
so much of social life is exhausting.*
—Anne Morrow Lindbergh

Why not go out on a limb? Isn't that where the fruit is?
—Frank Scully

I can resist anything but temptation.

You're only as happy as your unhappiest child.

Men are about status. Women are about connection.

It's not about IQ. It's about I will.

*Charity should be measured not only by what you
give, but by what you have left after you give!*

*If you touch a thistle, it will prick you. If you
grab it by the spine, it will crumble.*

When you lie down with dogs, you wake up with fleas.

IF is half of lIFe.

You never go wrong doing the right thing.

It's better to be lucky than smart.

A camel is a horse designed by a committee.

*Focus on the things over which you
have Input, Impact, and Control.*

CHAPTER 14
Random Topics and/or Pet Peeves

Twenty-five years ago, after I finished *How To Succeed in Life: Ideas and Principles They Don't Teach in School*, I approached a few agents about representing me and promoting the book. They said, "The first thing you have to do is write a 30-page paper about why you wrote the book!" I thought to myself:

- No, I don't. If you read the one-page Introduction, you'll see why I wrote the book!
- I'll form my own publishing company and do it "my way"!

So I formed Diamond Publishing Company and created my own cover design and choose its color, my own font sizes and my own layout. I did it "my way" and have been very pleased with the results.

Why "Diamond" Publishing?

- I love baseball and it's played on a DIAMOND.
- I'm a huge Neil DIAMOND fan.
- I love the "Acres of DIAMONDS" story.

Some "things" don't change over a quarter of a century. My attitude, philosophy, and way of navigating my life are three of those non-negotiable "things" that don't change. As I was finishing this book, I had breakfast with a friend. He noticed that I ate the crust of my bread and left the bulk of the bread uneaten. He commented, "Most people eat the inside and leave the crust." I replied, "I'm not like 'most people' . . . never have been; never will be."

Given that brief historical background, I am giving myself permission to opine about random topics and pet peeves. No apologies are necessary.

"HOW ARE YOU?" AND "HAVE A NICE DAY"

Both of these trite expressions are grossly overused and annoying. I understand that they are commonplace pleasantries and serve a social purpose. That doesn't stop them from being annoying. And you don't HAVE a nice day, you MAKE a nice day.

"HOW'S THE WORLD TREATING YOU?"

This question is like asking the fireplace to give you heat and THEN you'll put in the wood. The world works the same way. The world doesn't care. If you present the world with a positive attitude and do nice things for everyone you encounter, the world will treat you accordingly. It's the law of cause and effect. If you treat the world well, it will treat you well. It's that simple.

SMALL TIPPERS

I know people who proudly proclaim their wealth and boast of their personal assets. Yet, at restaurants, they will actually calculate a 15% tip to the exact penny! It would make absolutely no difference to them or their standard of living if they gave their server an extra $1, $5, or even $10! They might even feel good about having performed a Random Act of Kindness (RAOK!) that would be significant to the deserving recipient.

SECRETS

If you have a secret that you don't want anyone else to know, don't tell anyone! Similarly, if someone wants to share a secret with you, but doesn't want you to tell anyone else, suggest to them that they not tell you in the first place. That way it's impossible for you to pass on the secret!

"CAN'T" DOESN'T EXIST

How often have you heard someone say: "I can't sell my house!" They are wrong. Because "can't" doesn't exist. My thought is simply, "You can sell your house very quickly. At the moment, you're just asking too much money. If you asked $1 for your house, you would sell it immediately. So somewhere between your current asking price and $1, you can sell your house." You may not get what you THINK the house is worth, but you CAN sell your house! The open market fairly determines the fair price between a willing seller and a willing buyer. This example is a frequent, obvious example.

Please . . . don't tell me, "I can't sell my house" or I "can't" anything. Most important, remember "can't" doesn't exist.

TIP OF THE ICEBERG THEORY

When we look at other people (family, friends, acquaintances, movie stars, sports heroes), rosy lifestyle pictures are usually portrayed. We see, or are shown, all the "good" things: fame, fortune, cars, jewelry, opulent living. We all have a public persona; be careful not to assume everything is as it appears on the surface.

What you aren't told, and don't see, are all the things beneath the visible surface, under "the tip of the iceberg:" their intimate private lives; family issues; unseen liabilities offsetting the visible assets; medical problems; addictions; etc.

Here's a vivid example. Many years ago, my wife and I had a lovely evening with good friends. When we got home, we commented about what a great couple they were. The next day we saw the wife. She took us aside and said there was something they hadn't told us the previous evening. We both assumed she was going to tell us, "I'm pregnant!" Instead, we were shocked to hear, "We're getting a divorce." All that glitters is not gold. Others may appear to "have it all." As "The Tip of the Iceberg Theory" proves, it's not necessarily so.

"STUFF"

I have an automobile license plate that says: "Lesz Mor." This motto is so true. We spend half our lives accumulating "stuff"; the other half trying to get rid of it!

We all have too much "stuff," more than we know and more than we can ever use or wear. We have so much stuff that it doesn't always fit in the available spaces. Many people pay considerable sums to store it. After a while we don't even know what we're storing.

I have a friend who moved to Cleveland 10 years ago and has stored "stuff" ever since. If she's paying only $100 a month for her storage unit, she has now spent $12,000! Think about it. It's been sitting in storage for 10 years. Three things are obvious. She:

- Is spending a lot of money.
- Doesn't use or need this "stuff."
- Likely doesn't remember what's being stored.

My basic philosphy is:

- Use it or toss it.
- When in doubt, throw it out.
- What would my kids do with this?

Here is my suggestion on how to clean out closets, basements, attics, and storage units. Instead of selectively picking individual items and deciding, one by one, what to discard:

- Remove everything from the closet.

- Promise yourself that you will only return half of what you took out. The other half will be given away.

Following this process, you will accomplish three things. You will have:

- Reduced your "stuff" by 50%, a notable accomplishment.
- Unburdened yourself from things you don't remember, don't need, and don't want.
- Given away many items to those who will happily use them.

And once this unnecessary "stuff" is gone, it will soon be forgotten.

CONFLICT RESOLUTION

Regardless of who we are, or what our stage in life (our age, our health, our family, etc.), we all experience stressful situations. They are facts of life. The issue is: How do we resolve them in the most efficient, effective manner? Here are some inherently stressful situations and specific suggested solutions.

Problem: A parent has two young children who may, quite naturally, disagree with each other about which TV show to watch, who gets to sit on which seat in the car, or who gets to push the elevator button. Clearly not life or death situations, but very meaningful to the kids, and matters that cause both parents and children great frustration.

Solution: This worked with our kids. Jenny was born on May 13th, an ODD day. Adam was born on January 20th, an EVEN day. Whenever there was a choice to be made . . . Jenny got to decide on odd days . . . Adam got to decide on even days. Not rocket science but most effective. Each child knew the rules, and there were never any more arguments. Simplistic Solution to a Complex Problem.

Problem: A parent dies leaving tangible property (jewelry, household goods, antiques, automobiles, etc.) to distribute to two adult children. The children can't agree on "who gets what." Sound familiar?

Solution #1: Flip a coin. The winner gets first choice of ALL items, no matter the size, shape, financial or psychological value. Then the other sibling gets the next two choices. This alternating process continues until all wanted items have been disbursed. The balance is donated to charity.

Solution #2: Flip a coin. The winner divides all items into two piles. The loser then selects which pile s/he wants. Obviously, knowing the loser gets to pick which pile he/she wants, the winner will make the two piles as even as possible! No disagreements, no arguments, no expensive legal fees, no lengthy court battles, and a reasonably prompt resolution!

Problem: Parents die leaving 50% ownership of a valuable vacation property to two children. Both children want this unique parcel for which each has fond childhood memories. Clearly, it is not practical to cut the house in half, and neither wants to be a joint owner with the other.

Solution #1: Flip a coin. The winner (Child A) determines the value of the property. The loser (Child B) decides whether s/he wishes to purchase, or sell, the property at the price determined by the winner. The loser has to carefully consider the value of the house and establish a "fair and reasonable" price. Why? Let's assume the property is appraised at $250,000.

> If A prices the house at $200,000, B will know $200,000 is below market price and will decide to be the buyer.

> If A prices the house at $300,000, B will know $200,000 is above market price and will decide to be the seller.

There may be other intangible issues involved here (ego, control, emotion, jealousy, sibling rivalry). You can easily understand how this emotional issue could cause both parties great stress and potentially "go on forever"! This simple solution would resolve the matter with no disagreements, no arguments, no expensive legal fees, and no lengthy court battles.

Solution #2: The two children conduct an auction between themselves. How? Simple. The two parties agree to predetermined ground rules. A binding legal document is prepared and executed. The document specifies when and how the proceeds will be paid by the buyer to the seller. Left blank are the name of the buyer, the name of the seller, and the eventual sales price. These three items will be filled in after the auction.

Each child is then given a deck of 3 x 5 cards with ever-increasing sales prices on the face of each one. For example, the cards would start at $25,000 and increase by $25,000 up to $200,000. On the back of each card are the words "buy" and "sell." Each child circles each of her cards either "buy" or "sell" at that specific amount.

Then the auction begins. The cards are placed, face down, on the table. Each participant turns over one card at the same time. When one child has marked a card "buy" and the other child has marked the card with the same price "sell," the auction is over. The buyer, the seller and the price have been determined in the fairest way imaginable. No disagreements, no arguments, no expensive legal fees, no lengthy court battles and a prompt resolution! Simplistic Solution to a Complex Problem.

From my own experience, I can attest to the value, the efficiency, and the effectiveness of the "auction" resolution. In 1990, I was 50% owner of a business. After 22 years as equal partners, both owners agreed that it was time for us to go our separate ways. But we could not agree on who was going to buy the business, who was going to sell the business, and at what price. After several months of conflict, legal expenses, tension, disagreement, and stress, we finally agreed to conduct an auction. It worked perfectly. Within about an hour, a willing buyer, a willing seller, and the fair market value of the business were all determined. The conflict and stress were instantly resolved. We shook hands, parted ways, have very rarely seen each other since, and "have lived happily ever after." Simplistic Solution to a Complex Problem.

CLOSING THE SALE

There's an old adage: "You don't ask . . . you don't get!" This is the basic problem: Many salespeople prepare lengthy, artistic presentations, but forget the most important aspect: asking the prospect to buy! You always wanted to have a date with that "special someone," but never mustered the courage to call, email, or text and ask! It's up to us to ask the important questions and take the necessary steps to help us live the life we're imagining. What's the downside?

POLITICS

Politics today is ubiquitous and highly contentious. I'm not touching this emotional subject but these quotes may put a smile on your face!

> *Nothing is so permanent as a temporary*
> *government program.*
> —Milton Friedman

> *Giving money and power to government is like*
> *giving whiskey and car keys to teenage boys.*
> —P.J. O'Rourke

> *Politicians are the same all over. They promise*
> *to build a bridge even where there is no river.*
> —Nikita Khrushchev

*Political reformer: one who wants
his chance at the trough.*
—Malcolm Forbes

*The only difference between death and taxes is that
death doesn't get worse every time Congress meets.*
—Will Rogers

MEMORY

Memories are complicated and confusing assets. When we reflect on our lives and the events we have experienced, do we remember:

- What actually happened?
- What we think happened?
- What we wish had happened?

An interesting rhetorical question to ponder. I'm not sure which answer is correct. Might be a bit of all three?

*Nothing is more responsible for 'the good
old days' than a bad memory.*
—Franklin P. Adams

EXPERTS

My favorite humorous definitions of an expert:

- A person who comes from more than 100 miles away.

- Someone who knows 60% more than the other people in the room.
- An "ex" is a "has-been." A "spurt" is a drip under pressure!

REGRETS

As much as we regret having regrets, we all have them. They are a normal fact of life for all of us human beings. Hopefully, they are not significant and are few and far between. Perhaps some of them could have been avoided. Who knows? Perhaps, regrets inform our tomorrows so that we can minimize them in the future.

We never know how we will look back on today's decisions and wish we had done something differently. One of the best ways to minimize potential regrets is to "make errors of commission rather than errors of omission."

One of my most memorable "acts of commission" occurred when I consciously decided to "retire" from tennis and spend as much time as possible watching my beautiful children grow up. Now 40 years later, I am thrilled with my "act of commission" and have absolutely no regrets!

Conversely, my biggest lifetime regret and "error of commission" is the poor choice I made about where to attend college. Quite simply, I hated almost every minute of my initial two and a half year experience before I finally transferred. If I had to do it over again, I would obviously make a different choice.

I often overlook the very obvious reality that we don't have "rewind" on this planet and, even if we did have "rewind," we couldn't "redo" any one life event without it totally changing everything else that came afterward.

My regrettable college experience was a necessary prerequisite for every single life event that has followed. Without that one major regretful experience, I would never have enjoyed all the love, happiness, and special existence with which I have been blessed. I would not have:

- My two special children and four wonderful grandchildren.
- My rewarding professional career.
- My unique sports experiences.
- All the specific people, events and memories that have made my life so special.

♦ ♦ ♦

My daughter-in-law Candy was a professional golfer on the LPGA tour for eight years. A native of Brazil, Candy was asked by a friend if she would be interested in representing Brazil in the 2016 Rio Olympics? Candy said, "I'm flattered, but I'm four months pregnant and have a two-year-old daughter. In addition, it would be an expensive undertaking. I'd need a full-time nanny, travel expenses, golf lessons, and fitness training sessions. It would be a huge commitment for me and my husband." Her friend suggested that

Candy discuss the opportunity with Adam. If she were committed to the undertaking, she should create a budget and he would consider underwriting her expenses.

When Candy did discuss it with Adam, he asked her, "If this were your daughter, what would you tell her?" Candy said, "Go for it!" So Adam said, "Let's do it." The costs were determined, and the friend agreed to fund the effort. Candy spent two years of dedicated hard work, time, and energy in an effort to achieve a lifelong ambition . . . to play golf in the Olympics in her hometown.

Unfortunately, Candy narrowly missed qualifying for one of the two Brazilian positions. She was obviously and justifiably sad she didn't "make it." But she will forever have the satisfaction of knowing she gave it her all. She has no regrets. If she hadn't undertaken this herculean effort (at age 35 and having been retired for eight years!), at some future time, she would likely look back and regret that in 2014 she had made an irrevocable "error of omission."

My worst "error of omission" occurred way back on March 2, 1962. I was a college freshman and thought I would travel the short distance to nearby Hershey, Pennsylvania, to see the Philadelphia Warriors play the New York Knicks. At the last minute, for whatever reason, I decided not to go. Imagine my surprise the next morning when the newspaper headlines read: "Wilt Scores 100!" The legendary Wilt Chamberlain had scored 100 points. It never happended before; it has never happened since. It was a unique moment in sports history, and I missed it. A historical error of omission that has served as a memorable lesson. Just Do It: Make errors of commission rather than errors of omission!

PRENUPTIAL AGREEMENTS

I'm not a lawyer and don't know the legal technicalities of "prenups." Generically, they are agreements that are executed before a marriage that clearly spell out what happens if "we agree to disagree." Given this country's 40–50% divorce rate, prenups seem to be very practical documents that should be at least considered before marriage.

We enter into marriage with the desire and intent of "until death do us part." Hopefully, that is the case. It is quite understandable that people might feel that a prenuptial agreement adds a very unsettling, business-like aspect to the impending marriage. And it very well could. Nevertheless, I'm a big proponent.

Hopefully, you'll be on the right side of the marriage statistics and never need to use a prenup. What's the downside? Better to make errors of commission than error of omission!

BASICS OF BASEBALL

For an entire lifetime (since age 8!), I have been, and still am, a huge baseball fan, the details of which are fodder for its own lengthy book. To coin a phrase: "Baseball has been very good to me!"

As with everything else in life, the game of baseball, and the business of baseball, have undergone dramatic and dynamic changes. Today's baseball "bible" is built on "analytics." Analytics has become the end-all and the be-all! Nothing is considered or implemented without major "analytics" input.

Perhaps analytics overlook the human elements of the game and don't place enough emphasis on "the basics":

- Baseball is a simple game made complicated by those who play it.
- Most games are lost, not won.
- To win, a team must throw the ball, catch the ball, hit the ball.

Without using complicated algorithms, here is Ned's ".571" rule: THE most basic math requiring no sophisticated analytics. The baseball season is a six-month-long, grueling marathon, requiring player endurance and perseverance over a weary 162 games schedule. And that's before you get to the playoffs. Essentially, each team plays seven games per week. If a team wins four and loses three, a .571 winning percentage, no avid fan, no casual observer, and no analytics guru, would get overly excited. But if a team finishes the regular season marathon with a .571 winning percentage, they will have won 92 games, almost certainly guaranteeing they will have won their division championship.

Another prominent philosophy is that homeruns are the most important offensive weapon. That may be the case, but I've always been a proponent of the old adages:

- A walk's as good as a hit.
- "Get 'em on, get 'em over, get 'em in."
- You might want to "bunt" against the shift. Not bunting is similar to turning down an intentional walk.

My own very elementary and fundamental "analytics" (simple math!) show that if a player gets one, just one, additional hit per week, he will get 26 more hits over the course of the season. Looking at three 2016 Cleveland Indians players:

- A .259 hitter would have been a .304 hitter.
- A .275 hitter would have been a .318 hitter.
- A .312 hitter would have been a .358 hitter.

Just one more hit per week has a dramatic impact on a player's batting average and significantly increases the team's chances of winning more games.

SPORTS ADAGES TO LIVE BY

- *"The ball game is never over until the last man is out."*
- *"Whether or not you play a sport, be one."*

- *It's not about winning or losing. It's about what you can control.* —Brad Stevens
- *"For when the One Great Scorer comes to mark against your name—he writes—not that you won or lost—but how you played the Game."* —Grantland Rice

♦ ♦ ♦

It is fitting to end this book with the very well known:

SERENITY PRAYER

God, grant me the serenity to accept things I cannot change;
Courage to change the things I can;
And wisdom to know the difference.

The Serenity Prayer is a synonym for:

Focus on the things over which you have Input, Impact, and Control.

Parting Thoughts

THERE ARE NO ORDINARY MOMENTS.

ENJOY EVERY DAY.

BE YOURSELF.

FOLLOW YOUR PASSION.

ACHIEVE YOUR POTENTIAL.

THREE ABSOLUTE REALITES

- You are never as young or healthy as you are today.

- No matter how much money you have, you can't buy time and you can't buy health.

- If you knew you weren't going to be here tomorrow, what would you do today?

HOW TO SUCCESSFULLY NAVIGATE THE FUTURE

Focus on the things over which you have Input, Impact, and Control!

Acknowledgements

All successful ventures require a significant team effort. I am blessed to have "surrounded myself with good people." Correction. Great people!

Thanks, in alphabetical order, to:

- Julie DiBiasio: Technical Support
- Phyllis Goldenberg: Editor
- Gray & Company: Publishing consultants
- Shelly Lazarus: Wife and Guiding Light
- Murphy & Co. Graphic Communications: Cover-Book Design
- Yopko Penhallurick, Marketing & Public Relations

Without your encouragement, support, ideas, suggestions, patience, dedication, invaluable professional assistance (background, knowledge, expertise, and experience), and most importantly, friendship and love, this book would not exist.

Special thanks to Jenny Dingle and Adam Grossman, my wonderful children, who are living proof that your Dad's philosophies and ideas are actually helpful in successfully navigating life in the 21st Century.

About the Author

I am not a "real" author, just a dedicated dad who wanted to pass along some ideas, thoughts, philosophies and experiences to my teenage children.

Twenty-five years ago, I published How to Succeed in Life, Ideas and Principles They Don't Teach in School. The results far exceeded any reasonable positive expectations. There have been eight printings with almost 50,000 copies in print. More dramatically, the psychological rewards have been "priceless." I'm extremely pleased and proud of these unbelievable results.

I was blessed to have had a fabulous, loving, supportive wife, Sheri. How good was she? Before we got married, my grandfather (who was a very astute judge of women) told me that there was only one thing wrong with her: "She's too good for you!" He was absolutely correct. Unfortunately, after thirty-eight years of marriage, and a five-and-a-half-year courageous battle with pancreatic cancer, Sheri passed away.

I am living proof that sometimes in life, it's better to be lucky than smart. I have been blessed twice. Today I am married to Shelly, a dynamic partner and a guiding light to me, to her family, and to a myriad of loving and appreciative friends, who are fortunate to benefit from her generous, wise counsel and guidance.

◆ ◆ ◆

For forty-five years, I was in the employee benefits consulting business, enjoying every day. I was extremely fortunate to have had a wonderful staff and loyal clients with whom it was a privilege to work. I worked hard, but I was not a "Type A" personality. With a reasonably compulsive fetish for organization and preparation, I was able to get things done in an efficient and timely manner, using these basic principles:

- Do Your Own Thing
- KISS—Keep It Simple Stupid
- Just Do It (My automobile license plate is JS DO IT.)

My parents gave me love, time, attention and a terrific education. I understand and appreciate that I was fortunate. I owned my own business. I did what I wanted, when I wanted. With a "family and fun come first" attitude, I was able to follow my passions and do the things I truly loved.

A friend told me, "I love and live your philosophy. You are my role model. You have your priorities straight. You do first things first. You're my hero. I want to be like Ned!"

If this "About the Author" intrigues you, perhaps you will enjoy this book. I hope so!

Made in the USA
Lexington, KY
28 July 2018